Early Canada

REVISED EDITION

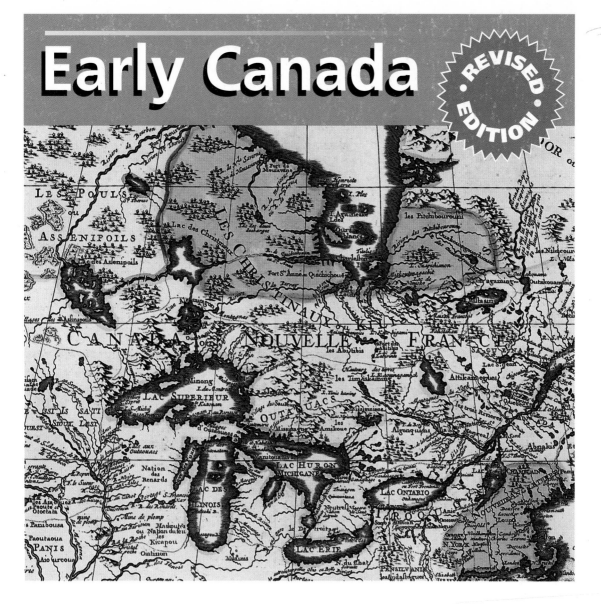

by Emily Odynak

Weigl

KANATA
THE CANADIAN STUDIES SERIES

Canadian Cataloging in Publication Data
        Odynak, Emily.
        Early Canada

        (Kanata)
        ISBN 0-919879-99-3

1. Canada—History—To 1763 (New France)—
Juvenile literature. 2. Canada—History—1763–1791—
Juvenile literature. I. Title. II. Series

FC161.O39 1998   j971.01   C97–911035–1
F1032.O39 1998

234567890 Printed in Canada 765432109

Acknowledgements

The publisher gratefully acknowledges the efforts of a
great many educators who were involved in the original
research and development of the Kanata Series under
the auspices of the Alberta Heritage Learning Resources
Project in 1980. Sincere thanks are extended to O.M.
Olineck, M.J. Werbitski, A. Petroskey, S.L. Tate, E.
Odynak, and to the County of Minburn No. 27.

Editorial Team for Original Edition
Edna Bakken, Sandra Bingaman, Catherine Edwards,
Lori Latta, Alan MacEachern, Cathie Pritchard, and
Maryanne Slater

Revised Edition

Editor
Lauri Seidlitz

Project Coordination and Copy Editing
Leslie Strudwick

Design
Warren Clark

Aboriginal Content Review
Bernie McKee has evaluated books for Alberta
Education for nine years. She has been a Tolerance and
Understanding analyst for five years.

KANATA
THE CANADIAN STUDIES SERIES

Canadian Families
Canadian Neighbours: How They Live
Special Canadian Communities
Links Between Canadian Communities
Early Canada
Cultures in Canada: Strength in Diversity
Les cultures au Canada: La force dans la diversité
Canada's Political Heritage: Conflict and Change
L'héritage politque du Canada: Conflits et changements
Canada in the World: Choosing a Role
Technology and Change in Canada
Citizenship in Action

Contents

Introduction

Who were the first people to live in what is now Canada? How did the land and its **resources** help them meet their needs? Why did people from Europe first come to Canada? When did they begin to **explore** Canada? When did they come to Canada to live? What happened when these newcomers met the **Aboriginal Peoples**? This book will help you answer these and other questions about the history of early Canada.

Early Canada has many special features to help you explore Canada's history. This introduction tells you about different kinds of information in this book. It explains how maps, pictures, and other types of **evidence** can help people discover and understand what happened in the past. The conclusion helps you review what you have learned about early Canada.

To learn the definitions of the words in **bold** type, look in the glossary near the end of the book. An index follows the glossary. If you want to find information about a person, place, or event in *Early Canada*, look in the index for the page number.

PART 1 "Aboriginal Peoples" begins with a map of Canada. The map shows where Aboriginal groups lived around the time the first Europeans came. Stories and pictures describe how Aboriginal Peoples such as the Mi'kmaq, Huron, Iroquois, and Cree lived at that time. This drawing by Lee Updike shows Huron women planting corn, squash, and beans.

PART 2 "Explorers" explains why explorers from Europe first came to Canada. It describes what they found and how the Aboriginal Peoples helped them. This painting shows the **voyage** of Jacques Cartier, an explorer who sailed up the St. Lawrence River in 1539.

PART 3 "Fur Traders" tells the story of Canada's fur trade. The **fur trade** began as a partnership between European traders and Aboriginal hunters. When the English and French began to compete for land and furs, the Aboriginal Peoples' way of life changed. This drawing shows a fur trader of the 1600s.

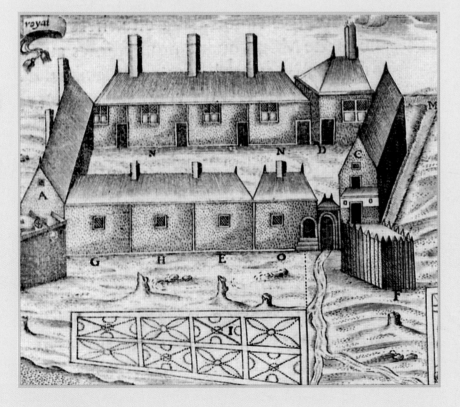

PART 4 "Missionaries" describes the work of Christian **missionaries** in early Canada. It explains how they interacted with the Aboriginal Peoples. In this picture, a **nun** is teaching children at a mission settlement.

PART 5 "Settlers" tells about the European **settlers** of Canada. It describes how the English and the French competed to control North America, and explains why Canada has two official languages. This drawing is a plan for Port-Royal, one of the first European settlements in Canada.

Learning about the Past

The journal written by Jacques Cartier, a European explorer, is an important record for historians. His journal describes the places he visited and the people he met.

This artifact was found by archaeologists near Lake Huron. It is a cooking pot that was used by Huron people around 1350.

How do new friends find out about you? They could talk to you or to people you know. They might look at pictures of you. Things you have written, such as letters, could give them more information.

Historians and **archaeologists** are people who study the past. They learn about past events and people in much the same way a stranger might learn about you.

Historians sometimes talk to people to learn about the past. For example, they may learn about the history of the Aboriginal Peoples by listening to their stories. Many stories have been told by Aboriginal parents to their children. When the children grow up, they tell the stories to their own children. Historians can learn about past events and people by listening to these stories.

Pictures can also tell historians about the past. Before there were cameras, people drew sketches of the people and places they saw. Some Aboriginal Peoples made pictures called **petroglyphs**. Early explorers and missionaries in Canada sketched and painted animals and plants that were new to them. They included themselves and their activities in their pictures, so we can learn about them as well as the places they visited. Some explorers drew pictures of the Aboriginal Peoples of Canada. The pictures showed Aboriginal Peoples' homes, tools, weapons, and clothing.

Many Europeans who came to early Canada kept journals of their trips. They often wrote letters to their families. They sent reports to their **monarchs**. Historians can learn about these early explorers and settlers and the places they visited from these **records**. Records are collected in **archives** and libraries so they can be studied.

Archaeologists study old objects rather than old records. Often objects have been buried in the ground for hundreds of years. These objects, called **artifacts**, tell archaeologists many things about the people who made and used them.

Learning about the past is a bit like doing a jigsaw puzzle. Pieces of information from different sources are fit together to form a picture. Sometimes pieces are missing, so the picture is not complete. Then people must try to guess what really happened.

Digging for the Past

Ten-year-old Jeff Jackson joined his mother for a day at work. Dr. Jackson is an archaeologist working at a site near Lake Huron. What does Jeff learn from his experience?

Jeff was surprised when he first saw the site where his mother was working, in a field beside a river. It was filled with big holes of different depths marked off by string squares. Several people were already working in the holes. Beside one hole were several small plastic bags containing pieces of broken clay pipes and some rusty metal fish-hooks.

"Fur traders smoked those pipes when they took breaks from paddling their canoes," said his mother. "They traded the hooks with the Aboriginal Peoples for furs."

Dr. Jackson gave Jeff a small shovel and paintbrush. "You can work on the lower level," she said. "Dig carefully with your shovel, and if you find something, uncover it gently with the brush."

Jeff worked eagerly for an hour, but he did not find anything. Just as he thought about getting a drink of water, his shovel hit something hard. He was excited, but he remembered to use his brush. Finally, he uncovered a black-coloured metal cross with a piece broken off one of its arms.

Jeff's mother came over to see what he had found. "It's a silver cross!" she exclaimed. "The date 1636 is scratched on it. The cross must have belonged to one of the missionaries who worked in this area." She called a photographer to take pictures of the cross before it was gently removed from the ground and labeled.

Jeff kept working at that spot for another hour. He found two stone arrowheads that he learned had been made by Aboriginal Peoples.

By then, Jeff was so hot, he needed to rest in the shade. "I'll find a cooler job for you," said his mother.

She took him over to a raised screen with a pile of dirt beside it. "Pour the dirt through the screen," she said. "See if you can find anything we missed while digging."

At first Jeff found nothing but rocks left on the screen. Then he noticed an object with an unusual shape. When he pushed the dirt away, he realized it was the missing piece from the cross he had found.

Before he went home that night, Jeff looked at the artifacts that had been found that day at the site. They proved that fur traders, missionaries, and Aboriginal Peoples had all visited the spot. People had used the area for more than three hundred years. It was a strange feeling to know that people so long ago, maybe even a boy his own age, had lived on the very spot where he was standing.

Learning from Maps

Maps are a source of useful information. They show the distances between places. They also show which parts of the world are water and which are land.

The earliest maps of Canada were drawn from memory. Certain Aboriginal people would memorize an area. When someone wanted to travel, the mapmakers drew the map in sand or snow. Sometimes they drew maps on bark or animal hides.

Explorers from Europe began making maps when they arrived in Canada. Many early explorers relied on the knowledge of the Aboriginal Peoples to help them. The earliest maps often showed only the coastlines. Empty spaces were left when the mapmaker did not know what features an area contained. As they travelled and learned more, the explorers added features to their maps, such as rivers, lakes, and mountains. As settlements were built, they were marked on maps. Trails and roads that settlers used appeared on maps as well.

Modern maps include all these features and more. They usually show the borders between provinces and countries. Mapmakers now use computers and images from satellites to make maps. Maps today usually look a lot different from old maps.

A map of Cartier's exploration of the St. Lawrence was drawn by Pierre Desceliers in 1546.

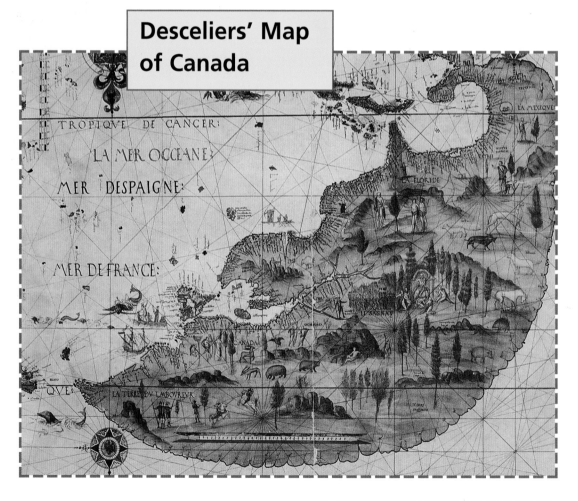

Desceliers' Map of Canada

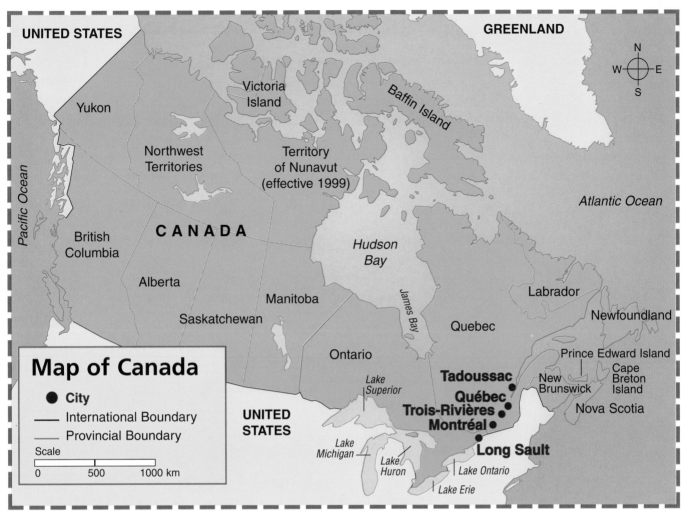

Map of Canada

- ● City
- ── International Boundary
- ── Provincial Boundary

Scale

| 0 | 500 | 1000 km |

UNITED STATES

GREENLAND

N
W   E
S

Yukon

Victoria Island

Baffin Island

Northwest Territories

Territory of Nunavut (effective 1999)

Atlantic Ocean

Pacific Ocean

C A N A D A

British Columbia

Hudson Bay

Alberta

Labrador

Manitoba

Saskatchewan

James Bay

Quebec

Newfoundland

Ontario

Prince Edward Island

Lake Superior

Tadoussac

New Brunswick

Cape Breton Island

Québec

Trois-Rivières

Nova Scotia

Montréal

UNITED STATES

Long Sault

Lake Michigan

Lake Huron

Lake Ontario

Lake Erie

Learning from Maps

What places do you recognize on Desceliers' map? Can you tell that his map is of the east coast of North America? Turn your book upside down–does it look more like the east coast now? Find Newfoundland on the map of Canada on page 9. Did Desceliers include Newfoundland on his map? Is the location of Newfoundland similar on both maps?

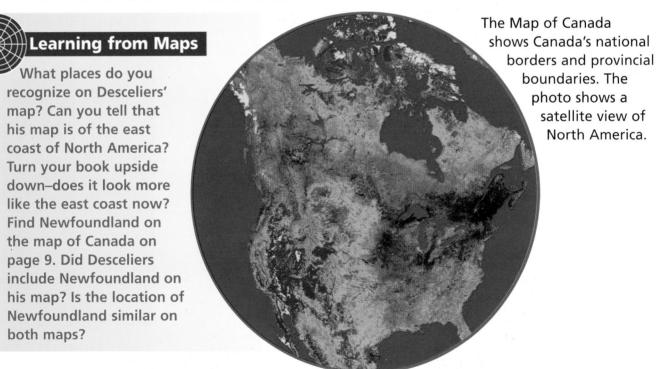

The Map of Canada shows Canada's national borders and provincial boundaries. The photo shows a satellite view of North America.

Learning from Time Lines

Events of the past can be shown on time lines such as the one below. Time lines can help you remember what you read. You may understand events better if you can see when one event happened compared to another. Each of the events in this time line is described in this book.

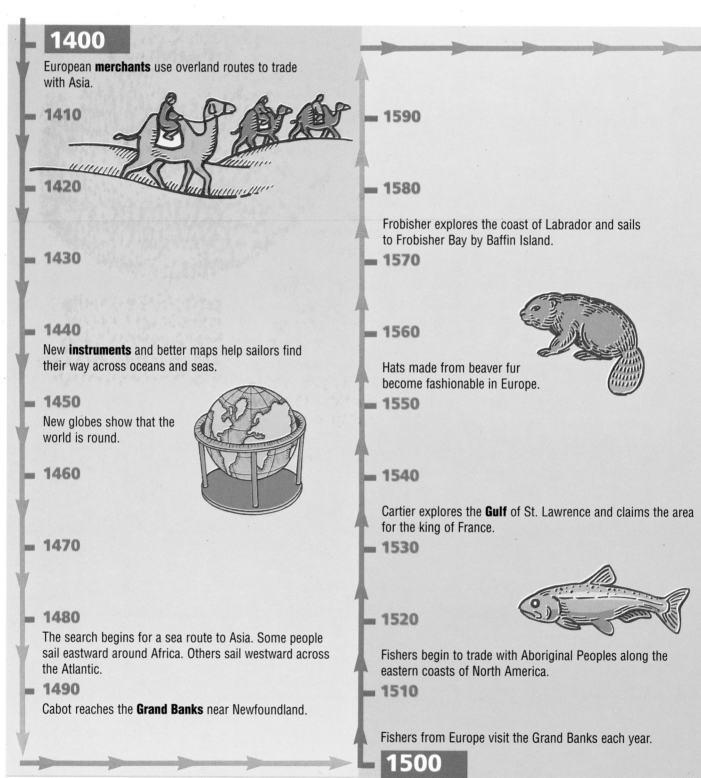

1400

European **merchants** use overland routes to trade with Asia.

1410

1420

1430

1440

New **instruments** and better maps help sailors find their way across oceans and seas.

1450

New globes show that the world is round.

1460

1470

1480

The search begins for a sea route to Asia. Some people sail eastward around Africa. Others sail westward across the Atlantic.

1490

Cabot reaches the **Grand Banks** near Newfoundland.

1590

1580

Frobisher explores the coast of Labrador and sails to Frobisher Bay by Baffin Island.

1570

1560

Hats made from beaver fur become fashionable in Europe.

1550

1540

Cartier explores the **Gulf** of St. Lawrence and claims the area for the king of France.

1530

1520

Fishers begin to trade with Aboriginal Peoples along the eastern coasts of North America.

1510

Fishers from Europe visit the Grand Banks each year.

1500

This time line shows the years from 1400 to 1800. During these years, Canada was explored and settled by people from Europe. This time line is divided according to centuries. A **century** is one hundred years long. A century is divided further into ten parts called decades. A **decade** is ten years long. Follow the arrows through the time line starting at 1400.

1600

The French start a settlement at Port-Royal. Champlain begins a settlement at Québec.

1610

Hudson sails into Hudson Bay. The Huron help Champlain explore inland areas. French farmers settle in the St. Lawrence River valley.

1620

Brébeuf and other missionaries come to Canada to teach Christian beliefs to the Aboriginal Peoples.

1630

French missionaries build a mission among the Huron. **Ursuline** nuns come to Québec.

1640

Ville-Marie is founded as a mission post on the island of Montréal. The French and English compete for control of the fur trade with their partners the Huron and Iroquois.

1650

Radisson and Groseilliers explore the area northwest of the Great Lakes.

1660

Groseilliers reaches Hudson Bay by sea to check whether it is a good fur-trading area.

1670

The Hudson's Bay Company is formed by the English.

1680

1690

Kelsey reaches the prairies and sees bison.

1800 to the present

Quebec is divided into two provinces: Upper Canada and Lower Canada.

1790

The American settlements become the United States. Some settlers from the United States move to Nova Scotia and the Great Lakes area.

1780

The Quebec Act lets French settlers keep their language, religion, and some of their laws.

1770

The Treaty of Paris ends the Seven Years' War. England takes control of eastern Canada.

1760

The English expel the French settlers in Nova Scotia. The Seven Years' War begins. The English destroy the French fortress at Louisbourg.

1750

France and England are at war during most of the 1740s and 1750s. The English build a **fortress** at Halifax.

1740

La Vérendrye begins to explore west of the Great Lakes and on to the prairies.

1730

1720

The **Treaty** of Utrecht gives England control over part of eastern Canada and the lands around Hudson Bay.

1710

The English attack French settlements on Canada's east coast.

1700

Part One

Aboriginal Peoples

The Aboriginal Peoples were the first people to live in North America. Groups of Aboriginal Peoples lived all over the continent. Each group had their own way of life, their own language, their own spiritual beliefs, and their own way to keep order. The way each Aboriginal group lived was linked to the kind of land on which they lived. Sometimes, more than one group shared a common language or way of life. Part One, "Aboriginal Peoples," looks at how four Aboriginal groups lived around the time Europeans came to North America. It describes where they lived, their daily life and beliefs, and the way they kept order. These Aboriginal Peoples were the first to meet the Europeans who arrived in the 1500s and 1600s.

The Ojibwa gathered wild rice that grew in the streams, lakes, and marshes of their homeland. They harvested the rice by knocking it off the plants into their canoes.

Sports and entertainment were part of the Aboriginal way of life. This drawing shows a **lacrosse** player. Lacrosse is a game that was first played by eastern Aboriginal Peoples.

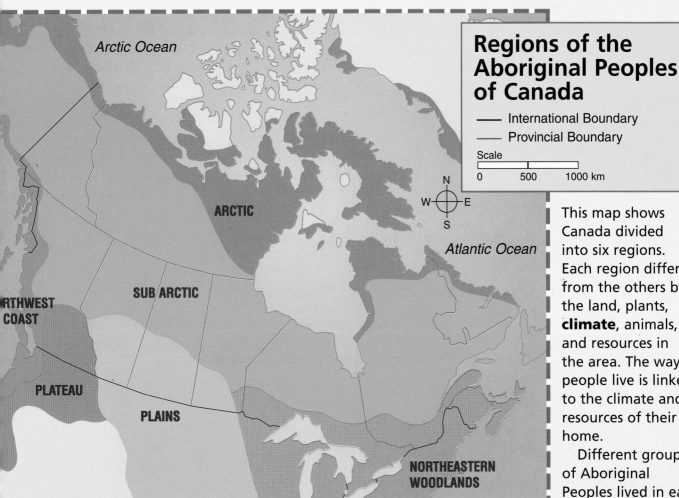

Regions of the Aboriginal Peoples of Canada

— International Boundary
— Provincial Boundary

Scale
0   500   1000 km

N W E S

Arctic Ocean

Atlantic Ocean

ARCTIC

SUB ARCTIC

NORTHWEST COAST

PLATEAU

PLAINS

NORTHEASTERN WOODLANDS

This map shows Canada divided into six regions. Each region differs from the others by the land, plants, **climate**, animals, and resources in the area. The way people live is linked to the climate and resources of their home.

Different groups of Aboriginal Peoples lived in each area. Many of them are part of the story of early Canada. The chart lists the Aboriginal Peoples who lived in each area around 1500, when Europeans first began coming to Canada.

Aboriginal Peoples of Canada

Arctic
Inuit peoples (Baffin, Caribou, Copper, Iglulik, Hudson Bay, Labrador, Mackenzie, Netsilik, Polar, Sadlermiut)

Subarctic
Algonquin, Dunne-za (Beaver), Beothuk, Dene (Chipewyan), Nehiyawak & Nihiyawak (Cree), Dogrib, Hare, Kutchin, Montagnais, Nahani, Naskapi, Ojibwa, Ottawa, Sekani, Dene Tha' (Slave), Tahltan, Yellowknife

Northeastern Woodlands
Erie, Huron, Iroquois Confederacy (Cayuga, Mohawk, Oneida, Onondaga, Seneca), Maliseet, Mi'kmaq (Micmac), Neutral, Petun, St. Lawrence Hochelagans and Stadaconans

Plains
Nakoda (Stony), Blackfoot Confederacy: Siksika (Blackfoot), Kainaiwa (Blood), Piikani (Peigan), Gros Ventre

Plateau
Carrier, Chilcotin, Interior Salish, Kootenay, Tagish, Tsetaut

Northwest Coast
Bella Coola, Coast Salish, Haida, Kwakiutl, Nootka, Tlingit, Tsimshian

Learning from Maps

Look at the map of Canada and pick one of the regions. What groups of Aboriginal Peoples lived in that region?

The First People of Canada

Thousands of years before Europeans explored and settled in Canada, Aboriginal Peoples made the land their home.

There are few written records to tell us about the **ancestors** of Canada's Aboriginal Peoples. Instead of written information, we learn about their lives from the things they left behind and from stories handed down through generations. Archaeologists study the tools and weapons that have been found buried in the earth. Old cooking pots and campsites can tell us about their day-to-day life.

Some people think that the ancestors of Canada's Aboriginal Peoples may have come from Asia. This idea is based on clues found by archaeologists. Pieces of bone, stone tools and weapons, and other objects found at sites in northeastern Asia and northwestern Canada are similar. Many archaeologists believe that Aboriginal groups immigrated from Asia 20 000 years ago when much of North America was covered by ice. At this time there was a land bridge between Siberia and Alaska. Some archaeologists believe the Aboriginal Peoples used this bridge to walk across to North America.

Many Aboriginal Peoples have different beliefs about their origins. They have explanations that describe how the land and their people were created long ago. They believe they originated in North America. These explanations are told by parents, grandparents, **elders**, and other relatives to younger generations. The explanations teach about the beliefs and customs of the Aboriginal Peoples.

The Siksika live in what is now Alberta. This Siksika maul is a heavy hammer or mallet. It was once used to pound or grind food.

The blade of this Siksika knife is made from elk horn and the handle is made from wood. It is bound together by leather.

How the Good Spirits Came to Rule the World

This Huron story is about how the world was created. Many traditional Aboriginal Peoples believe that stories such as this one should be told only in winter storytelling months and only by certain people. The story would be told in an Aboriginal language. Translating the story into English takes away some of the deeper meanings that Aboriginal languages and beliefs include.

Long, long ago, there was nothing but water everywhere. The only living beings were the water animals and birds.

In a spirit world far above the skies lived Sky-Man and Sky-Woman.

One day Sky-Man became very ill. Sky-Woman, who was going to have a baby, went into the forest. She wanted to get some medicine plants that would make her husband well. As she dug around the roots of a tree, she broke a hole in the sky.

Down, down she fell through this bottomless hole toward the water. Two loons flying over the water looked up. They could see Sky-Woman falling. Spreading their wide wings, the loons caught Sky-Woman and gently carried her down toward the sea below. While they carried her, the loons cried out for help to the other water creatures.

All the water animals rushed together as soon as they heard the loons call. Great Turtle ordered the creatures to swim to the bottom of the sea. One by one, each animal brought up some earth and piled it on top of Great Turtle's back.

Just in time, Great Turtle swam over to catch Sky-Woman. The loons dropped her on the soft earth piled on his back.

Sky-Woman spread the earth all over Great Turtle's shell to make dry land. The land continued to spread. Soon plants and trees began to grow.

Sky-Woman built herself a house under a large tree. She waited for her baby to be born.

Surprise! Sky-Woman had twin sons, but she did not live to see them grow up. She died and was buried in the earth. Her last gifts to the world were three special plants.

Corn, beans, and squash grew from her body. Later, people learned how to harvest these foods and to gather seeds for replanting.

As the two brothers grew up, they showed special powers. Each of the brothers gave the world something.

Flint, or Evil Brother, created giant snakes, fierce beasts, and huge insects to frighten and torment people. He also created **briers**, weeds, and plants that could be used for medicines or poisons.

Sapling, or Good Brother, created animals that were harmless and useful to people, such as caribou and bears. People could eat their flesh. They could use their bones and horns to make tools and weapons. They could use their skins and furs to make clothing. Sapling also made berries, fruits, and nuts for people to eat.

The brothers eventually realized they could not live in the same world. They held a duel to decide who would rule the world.

Flint beat his good brother with a bag full of corn and beans until Sapling lay on the ground, almost dead.

However, Sky-Woman's good spirit helped Sapling recover, and he stabbed his evil brother with a deer's antlers. Today, Sapling rules the sky and the world above the earth. Flint is master of the world beneath the earth.

The Mi'kmaq, A Coastal People

When the Europeans began to explore North America, the Mi'kmaq people lived on the east coast. Most lived in the areas now called Nova Scotia and Prince Edward Island. Others lived along the coast of New Brunswick. Later on, some Mi'kmaq moved to the Gaspé **Peninsula** in Quebec, and to Newfoundland. The Mi'kmaq were one of the first Aboriginal groups to meet the Europeans.

Many Aboriginal languages can be grouped in families of similar languages. One group is the **Algonquian** family. **Anthropologists** think that all the people who speak languages from the Algonquian family might share the same ancestors. The Mi'kmaq people spoke an Algonquian language, as did their closest neighbours, the Abenaki and Maliseet.

The land where the Mi'kmaq lived was covered by forests. There were many rivers and streams running into the ocean. Although the climate was difficult, with harsh storms in the winter, the Mi'kmaq were able to use the rich resources of both land and water. The ocean, rivers, and forests played an important part in the way the Mi'kmaq people lived.

The boxed area on this map shows where the Mi'kmaq people lived around 1500. This area is in the Northeastern Woodlands.

Learning from Maps

Find the Mi'kmaq on the chart on page 13. What other groups lived in the Northeastern Woodlands?

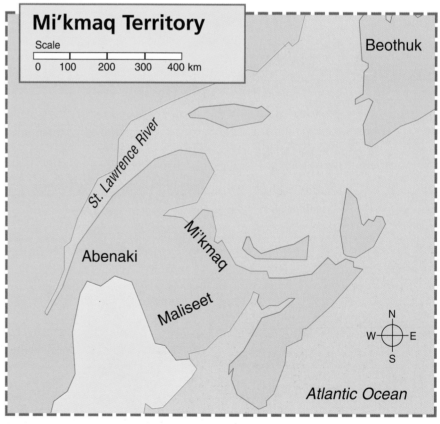

Mi'kmaq Territory

Scale

0   100   200   300   400 km

St. Lawrence River

Beothuk

Abenaki

Mi'kmaq

Maliseet

N
W   E
S

Atlantic Ocean

The Daily Life of the Mi'kmaq

The Mi'kmaq people moved from place to place as the seasons changed. In the winter, they moved inland to the forests. They hunted beavers, moose, bears, and caribou. In the spring, they moved to the coast. They fished in the ocean and rivers for fish and shellfish, and they hunted sea animals. Sometimes they caught seals and small whales. They hunted seabirds, and looked for their eggs.

Most of the Mi'kmaq's food came from the sea. They fished with hooks and lines, nets, or harpoons. The Mi'kmaq built fishing **weirs** in the water. Weirs are large traps built of wooden poles. The fish would swim into the weirs and then the Mi'kmaq could net or spear them easily.

The Mi'kmaq men fished and hunted for large animals. The Mi'kmaq women fished, trapped smaller animals, and gathered wild plants for food. The women prepared the food for eating. Sometimes they boiled meat by dropping hot stones into water. They also prepared food for storage by drying or smoking it.

Because the Mi'kmaq moved around with the seasons, they needed light houses that could be carried to new places. They lived in light, bark-covered **wigwams**. There were different sizes and shapes of wigwams, depending on the size of a family. The wigwams were decorated with coloured designs.

The Mi'kmaq made their clothes from hides and fur. They decorated their clothes with moose-hair embroidery and designs made from porcupine quills.

Feasts were held to mark important events such as marriages. The feasts were a time to tell stories, play games, sing, and dance. Sometimes, the Mi'kmaq held feasts before going on hunting trips.

In the winter, the Mi'kmaq would use snowshoes to walk on top of the deep snow. They used sleds and toboggans to carry their things from place to place. The word "toboggan" comes from a Mi'kmaq word.

The Mi'kmaq travelled in light birchbark canoes along the coast and up rivers and streams. Each canoe was big enough to hold a whole family and all their goods. The picture shows a Mi'kmaq canoe shaped so ocean waves cannot get in. The Mi'kmaq made many things from birchbark, such as wigwams, baskets, and bowls.

Mi'kmaq Beliefs

The Mi'kmaq people shared similar beliefs with the other people who spoke Algonquian languages. They lived in close harmony with nature. They thought there was a single creator of the world. They believed that all plants and animals had spirits. Spirits also lived in places like waterfalls.

The Mi'kmaq had many stories they used to teach their beliefs and customs. One of their favourite heroes was named Glooscap. Many stories tell how Glooscap made the animals and natural features of the land. Other stories tell how he taught human beings to make tools and weapons.

The spiritual leaders of the Mi'kmaq people were called **shamans**. They performed spiritual ceremonies and they cared for people who were ill.

Keeping Order

The Mi'kmaq lived together in groups. During the winter months, only a few families lived together. In the summer, when it was easier to find food, several hundred people joined together to form a **band**.

Each band had a chief called a sagamore. The sagamore gave leadership and advice to the band. When a sagamore died, his place was taken by his son if the people thought the son would make a good leader. There was one grand chief of the Mi'kmaq, who lived on Cape Breton Island. The grand chief sometimes called all the sagamores together to discuss problems.

The Mi'kmaq people believed they were protected by spirit guardians. They believed their spirit guardians would help them make the right decisions. Spirit guardians were sometimes animals familiar to the Mi'kmaq such as caribou, moose, and bears.

Iroquois and Huron Farmers in the Great Lakes Area

When Europeans began to explore the St. Lawrence River valley, they met the Iroquois and Huron people who lived in the Great Lakes **Lowlands**. These people spoke languages from the **Iroquoian** language family.

The Iroquois were a nation of five Aboriginal groups who had joined together in a **league**. The members of the League of the Iroquois were the Seneca, Oneida, Mohawk, Cayuga, and Onondaga. In the 1700s, they were joined by a sixth group, the Tuscarora, who lived farther south. They formed what is now one of the oldest democratic societies in the world.

The home of the Huron was on a **peninsula** in Georgian Bay, on Lake Huron. Huron was the name given to them by the French. The French called their homeland Huronia. In their own language the Huron called themselves *Wendat*, which means "islanders" or "dwellers on a peninsula."

The way the Huron and Iroquois people lived was related to the land, climate, and resources of their area. The Great Lakes Lowlands had rich soil that was good for growing crops. It had a climate suited for agriculture, with a summer long enough for many plants to grow. There were large forests where they could hunt. Some trees were cut down to make room for fields where they could grow food. As well as farming and hunting, they fished in the Great Lakes and hunted in the forests. Because their area had many resources, people lived close together. They did not need to spread out and travel around to find food.

The large map shows where the Huron and the Iroquois lived around 1600. The smaller map shows that this area is part of the Northeastern Woodlands.

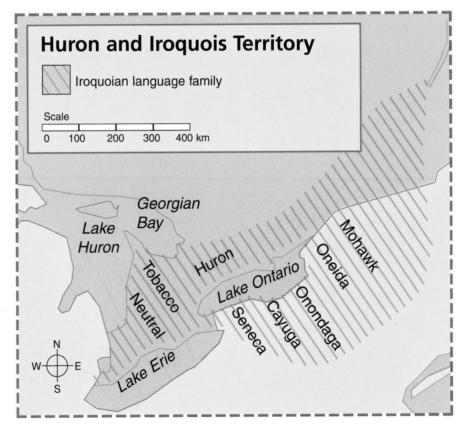

Huron and Iroquois Territory

Iroquoian language family

Scale
0 100 200 300 400 km

Georgian Bay
Lake Huron
Tobacco
Neutral
Huron
Lake Ontario
Mohawk
Oneida
Onondaga
Cayuga
Seneca
Lake Erie

N W E S

Month	Temp (°C)	Rain/ Snow (mm)
January	-5°	99
February	-6°	76
March	-1°	74
April	6°	74
May	12°	71
June	18°	66
July	20°	81
August	20°	79
September	16°	99
October	9°	86
November	3°	89
December	-4°	109

Corn needs about 120 frost-free days to grow and ripen. Corn plants also need more than sixty-five millimetres of rain each month during the growing season.

Finding Information

1. Use the information on the chart to find the three best months for growing corn.

2. How can you tell which months are best?

Longhouses were usually from forty-five to fifty-five metres long and about eleven metres wide.

The Daily Life of the Huron and Iroquois

The Huron and Iroquois were farming people. They grew most of their own food in the summer months.

They lived in villages. Some of the villages were large, with many people. Several families lived together in bark-covered longhouses. Inside there was room for several cooking fires and many sleeping platforms. Longhouses had room to store food, weapons, clothing, and tools. Often dried foods were hung from the ceiling. There were storage porches at each end. Items such as dried corn were stored in pits dug into the earth floor.

Women planted and raised the crops. They also did the cooking and gathered nuts and berries in the woods near their homes. They made clothing, and clay and wooden containers. They also looked after the children. Men cleared the fields and made canoes, tools, and weapons. They also hunted and fished and protected the villages from harm. The men travelled to visit other Aboriginal groups to trade their extra food for furs, hides, and other goods.

The Huron and Iroquois made their clothing from deer hides and beaver **pelts**. Clothes were decorated with painted or porcupine quill designs. Bracelets, necklaces, and earrings were made from shell beads. The women wore their hair in a single braid, but the men had several different hairstyles. Some shaved the sides of their head, leaving a strip of hair down the middle. Others shaved only one side of their head and left long hair on the other.

The Huron and the Iroquois did not travel as much as the Mi'kmaq. They sometimes went on fishing and hunting trips, or travelled to trade with other groups. They used birchbark canoes in the summer and snowshoes in the winter.

They held feasts with dancing and games to celebrate special occasions. Lacrosse, for example, was a popular game played with rackets and balls. Teams from different villages often competed against one another.

Moving to a New Village

This story tells about some important events in the lives of a group of Huron people. Which work was done mostly by men? Which work did women do? What part did children play in these events?

Toca and Sondaqua, the ten-year-old twins of a Huron chief, ran ahead of the others along a pathway through the forest. They stopped at the edge of a huge clearing. This was the spot for their new village.

The clearing was near a curve in a stream. Springs nearby would supply the village with drinking water.

Toca felt the rich, dark soil with her fingers. It would grow good corn. Sondaqua saw deer tracks that told him there would be game in the forest around the new village. The trees would provide bark for their new longhouses and firewood to cook their food and keep them warm.

The twins ran back to help their mother and the other Huron women from the village. The women carried babies and made sure household goods arrived at the new village safely. The men paddled loaded canoes up the stream to their new home.

Many things had to be moved from the old village to the new village. The people brought strong poles and pieces of elm and cedar bark for building new houses. They moved **mortars and pestles** for grinding corn, clay cooking pots, wooden bowls and spoons, and bark boxes filled with dried foods. There were many other items to be moved, from fur robes to bone needles.

Three years ago, Gahwonh-nos-da, the head woman of the village, had told the people that they should move. They had planted corn in the same fields for ten years. The soil was tired. The elders agreed.

They asked the young men to find a new place and to clear the land for corn fields.

Now it was time to move. Winter was over. The fields were ready. It would soon be time to plant the seeds that would grow in the warm sun.

The morning after the move, Toca was up early. She looked after the younger children while her mother helped the other men and women build their new longhouses. Sondaqua helped the men build a tall fence made of wooden poles around the village. They covered the fence with bark. Then they built look-out platforms along the inside of the **palisade**. From there, they could watch for any enemies that might come.

When the time was right, the women and children planted corn, beans, and squash in the new fields. Corn was an important food. Some would be dried and made into flour for cornbread. Some would be made into soup called **sagamité**. The women planted enough for all the people in the village and a little extra to trade with the neighbouring peoples.

While the women were planting, a group of men left the village to trade for furs and other goods with the Algonquian people who lived farther north.

In the fall, the traders returned to the village. They brought birchbark canoes, clay cooking pots, colourful beads, and warm furs. They had many stories to tell of the people they had met and the dangers they had faced.

Huron and Iroquois Beliefs

The Huron and Iroquois peoples believed that all things have a soul or spirit. Some of the spirits were good and some were bad. The most powerful spirits, such as the sky spirit, were called *oki*. Corn, beans, and squash were thought to have sister spirits.

The Huron and Iroquois believed they could understand the spirit world through their dreams. Sometimes a shaman helped explain the meaning of dreams.

Some of the oldest, wisest people were chosen to pass on traditions and stories about the past. These elders recited stories at feasts.

Keeping Order

The Huron and the Iroquois had different ways of keeping order. The Huron had two kinds of chiefs. One kind looked after everyday decisions in the villages. They kept order and settled disagreements. The other kind were war chiefs, who protected the villages. Each clan, or group of related families, had one of each kind of chief. If there were many clans, there would be many chiefs in a village. The chiefs were chosen because of their speaking skills, bravery, and wisdom.

Two councils looked after the affairs of each village. One council was made up of the chiefs and elders who looked after the affairs of the village. The other council was made up of chiefs who looked after the village's relations with other villages and groups of people. The council members tried to reach agreements that satisfied everyone. All the members could express their views. Once a year, there was a council of the Huron people. The village chiefs from all over Huronia met to renew their friendship and discuss matters of common concern.

The Iroquois formed a system to keep peace and order among its five members. Before the League of the Iroquois started, the groups sometimes fought with one another.

The league was governed by fifty chiefs called sachems. They met every August or September to discuss issues important to their people. The Iroquois used the idea of a longhouse to describe their league. The Onondaga, who lived in the middle of the Iroquois territory, were the "Keepers of the Fire" in the longhouse. The Seneca represented the western door of the longhouse, and the Mohawk the eastern door. At meetings, the sachems had a special place to sit according to their place in the longhouse. Because of their special position, the Onondaga were in charge of keeping the historical records of the league. The Onondaga chief was the head of the League of the Iroquois.

The sachems were all men. However, it was the women who chose the sachems to represent their people. They could replace a sachem if he did not do his job well.

The League of the Iroquois was made up of separate Aboriginal groups with their own interests and their own way of life. In council meetings, the leaders of each nation had to make speeches to explain their point of view to the other groups. While they made their speeches, they held a wampum belt, such as the one pictured here, as a sign of truth.

What do you think?

1. **How might the elders get everyone to find a solution to a problem?**

2. **How would you get people to agree on a solution to a problem?**

People with Different Ideas

A chief called Hiawatha may have helped start the League of the Iroquois. Hiawatha believed the words of the prophet Deganawida who spoke of a Great Peace among the Iroquois nations. Hiawatha helped convince the warring nations to join the Iroquois constitution. A woman named Jingosaseh made sure the constitution treated women equally. It must have been difficult to convince people to enter a partnership with groups with whom they had often disagreed. When Hiawatha spoke with these nations, he may have used an argument such as the one below.

AN IROQUOIS CHIEF

Why should my people associate with the group to the north, when all they do is make our lives difficult? Last summer they kidnapped three people from my own village, and now you want me to sit around a fire with them. You say you might even want me to go to war to protect them. If they get into a war with the Hurons, I'm sure they deserve it.

Anyway, who will be in charge of this league? Don't think my people will do whatever some Onondaga leader tells them. We are our own nation.

HIAWATHA

If your people join the League of the Iroquois, those to the north of you will be your friends, and there will be no more kidnapping. If you have a quarrel with them about land or trade, just bring your complaint to the council meeting. There will be many wise sachems there to discuss the problem. No decisions will be made until we come up with solutions upon which everyone will agree.

If any member of the league gets into a war that you don't agree with, you don't have to fight. However, if you are attacked by some other group, you can ask the league members to help you. Together, we will all be strong.

In what ways was the league organized so that people with different ideas would still be happy?
Do you think this made the league stronger or weaker? Why?

Cree Hunters of the Northern Forests

The boxed area on this map shows where the Cree people lived before Europeans came to North America. The Cree lived farther north than the Mi'kmaq, Huron, and Iroquois. Since the climate was colder, plants and animals were not as plentiful as in southern regions. The Cree needed a larger area to live so they could find enough food.

What do you think?

Because they lived farther north, in what ways might the Cree way of life be different from other groups' way of life?

Before Europeans came to North America, most of the Cree people lived mainly around James Bay and along the western shore of Hudson Bay, in the Subarctic area. This group is now called the James Bay Cree. Some Cree people also lived on the Prairies. They are now known as the Plains Cree.

The Cree spoke one of the languages from the Algonquian language family. It was similar to the Mi'kmaq language. The Cree and the Mi'kmaq also shared a similar way of life. They were both hunting peoples. There were differences in their way of life as well, because the Mi'kmaq were a coastal people and the Cree were a forest people.

The Subarctic area covers a large part of Canada. It is a low, rolling land of rocky forest. The soil is thin and poor. The winters are long and cold, and the summers are short. There are many lakes and rivers. Shrubs, berries, and mosses grow well in the forests. Not as many wild plants grow in the Subarctic forests as in the Northeastern Woodlands, so the Cree relied on hunting for their food.

The Daily Life of the Cree

The Cree hunted moose, caribou, bears, and beavers in the forests. They also trapped smaller animals such as hare, otter, mink, and red squirrel. The Cree who lived close to Hudson Bay and James Bay also fished and hunted sea animals such as seals and small whales. Wild geese and ducks were part of the Cree peoples' **diet**. During the summer, the Cree also picked berries.

The Cree lived in small hunting groups most of the time. Each group needed a large area in which to find enough food. Large groups of people living in one area might have exhausted the resources. Instead, there was balance.

In the summer, the Cree formed larger groups at good fishing spots. Sometimes they travelled to Lake Superior to fish with the Ojibwa people.

The Cree travelled in light birchbark canoes in the spring and summer. In the winter, they wore snowshoes and carried their goods on toboggans and sleds. Cone-shaped wigwams were their homes. The wigwams were often covered with caribou or moose hides for warmth. In some places, the Cree made winter houses of sod and earth packed over a framework of poles. The Cree made their clothing out of caribou or moose hides with designs made from quills.

People with Different Ideas

Different Aboriginal Peoples had different ways of life. The Mi'kmaq and the Cree followed a circular seasonal pattern in search of food. The Huron and Iroquois lived in one place so they could farm. The Cree and the Huron might have described their lives in the following way.

A CREE HUNTER

The thing I most enjoy is travelling in my canoe. I often go for long distances in search of moose or other animals. My family and I built the canoe ourselves out of bark. We repair it with spruce gum when necessary. It will carry us anywhere we want to go.

We usually travel with a few other families. We set up our wigwams close together. We choose the best hunter to be our leader. Our decisions are made by **consensus**.

Mainly we travel to find food. Sometimes we meet with other people to trade or visit. We never stay in one place very long.

A HURON FARMER

My favourite time of year is the fall, when my family and I harvest our crop of corn and squash. We usually have good crops, so there is enough food for us to eat and some left over to trade.

We live in a longhouse in a large village with hundreds of other people. There is a palisade around our village for protection. We don't need it very often, because our leaders can usually make peace with our neighbours.

We don't travel very much except to trade. We can get hides, canoes, and fish from neighbouring hunters in return for our vegetables. We only move to new homes when the land in one place has been planted for too many years and is no longer very good for crops.

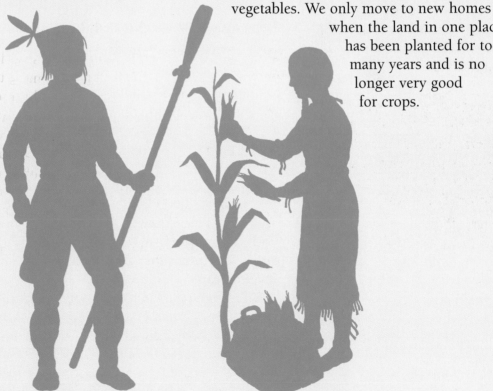

**Which way of life would you prefer? Why?
Why might people living differently come into conflict
with one another?**

Cree Beliefs

The Cree believed in a Great Spirit who looked after everything. They called this spirit **manitou**. There were also other spirit helpers who were often animals. The Cree had great respect for these spirits.

Cree hunters would pray to the Great Spirit for a good hunt. When hunters killed a moose, they would say a special thank you to the moose for giving up its life. Another animal that had powerful strength was the bear. When a bear was killed, a special feast was held. The skull of the bear was placed high in a tree so it could not be damaged by other animals.

The Cree people believed in helping one another. If one hunter killed a moose, it was always shared with others in the group. Elders were always given the best parts of the animal. Sharing was a way of life for the Cree people.

Keeping Order

On winter hunts, the best hunter and speaker was usually picked to be the leader. Everyone in the group helped make decisions for the group.

When several bands joined together in the summer, the same thing happened. The best speaker from the winter leaders was chosen to become the summer leader. The leader's main job was to deal with people outside the group. All important decisions were discussed by all the adults. Nothing was done until everyone agreed.

Moccasins are a type of shoe made of soft animal skin. They were worn by many Aboriginal Peoples. Each group had its own style and its own way of decorating their moccasins. This drawing shows a pair of Cree moccasins.

This painting shows a Cree family in their tent. Why might a Cree family choose to live in a wigwam rather than a longhouse?

In Summary

1. There are no written records left by the ancestors of Canada's Aboriginal Peoples. Archaeologists study artifacts to learn more about these first inhabitants of Canada. Aboriginal Peoples also have stories that tell about their ancestors and their culture.

2. Many different Aboriginal Peoples lived in North America when the first Europeans arrived. They lived in six geographic regions. The climate and geography of the land affected how each group lived.

3. Each group had its own way of life, spiritual beliefs, and way to keep order. Sometimes, people in the same area shared similar ways of life and similar languages.

4. The Mi'kmaq were a coastal people who lived on Canada's east coast. The Huron and the Iroquois were farmers near the Great Lakes. The Cree were hunters in the northern forests.

Reliving the Past

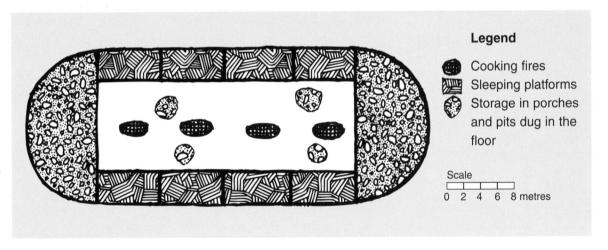

Legend

- Cooking fires
- Sleeping platforms
- Storage in porches and pits dug in the floor

Scale
0 2 4 6 8 metres

This drawing shows the floor plan of a Huron longhouse.

1. Use the symbols in the legend to find where cooking was done, where families slept, and where food was stored.

2. Use the scale to answer these questions:
   - How many metres long is the longhouse?
   - How many metres wide is the longhouse?

3. Measure a rectangle outside your school or in your gymnasium that is the same size as the longhouse. Mark the edges with chalk or string. Mark the areas where the sleeping platforms and cooking fires would be.

4. Explain how life for families in the longhouse would have been different from the way you live.

Part Two

Explorers

Have you ever moved to a new city, gone to a wilderness camp, or visited a friend in another town? While you were there, did you discover interesting things to see? Did you meet new people? Did you have to learn how to find your way in a strange place?

If you have done any of the above, you were learning about the unknown. You were an explorer. An explorer is a person who searches for information about unknown places.

Part 2, "Explorers," describes some of the first European explorers who came to Canada. Europeans began to look for a new water route to Asia in the 1400s. They wanted to trade for **spices**, silks, and jewels in the countries of Asia.

The 1400s were exciting years in Europe. People's ideas about the world were changing. New instruments were invented to guide sailors on long sea voyages. Better sailing ships were built with more space for supplies and **crew**. Trade with other countries made people want to explore the unknown.

The land route from Asia to Europe was long and dangerous. It was also expensive. Goods had to be moved using camel caravans across mountains and deserts.

The route by water was not much better. Goods were taken to ports on the Mediterranean Sea and loaded onto ships. The ships sailed around the southern tip of Africa to Asia. The ports on the Mediterranean Sea were controlled by Italian cites that charged high **tolls** to people from other countries. The water route south of Africa was especially dangerous.

Many explorers thought they could find a route to Asia by sailing west across the Atlantic Ocean. Instead of Asia, they found North America. For a long time, explorers tried to sail around or find a passage through North America. They called the route they were looking for the **Northwest Passage**.

When they reached North America, they found a rich fishing ground. The explorers met Aboriginal Peoples who taught them many things about the new land and guided them on their trips. The Aboriginal Peoples began to trade furs with the Europeans for tools, clothing, and weapons. The Europeans learned that North America had many rich resources.

Finding Information

1. What advantages and disadvantage were there to overland trading routes and water trading routes?

2. If you were an English merchant in 1500, would you choose a land or water trading route?

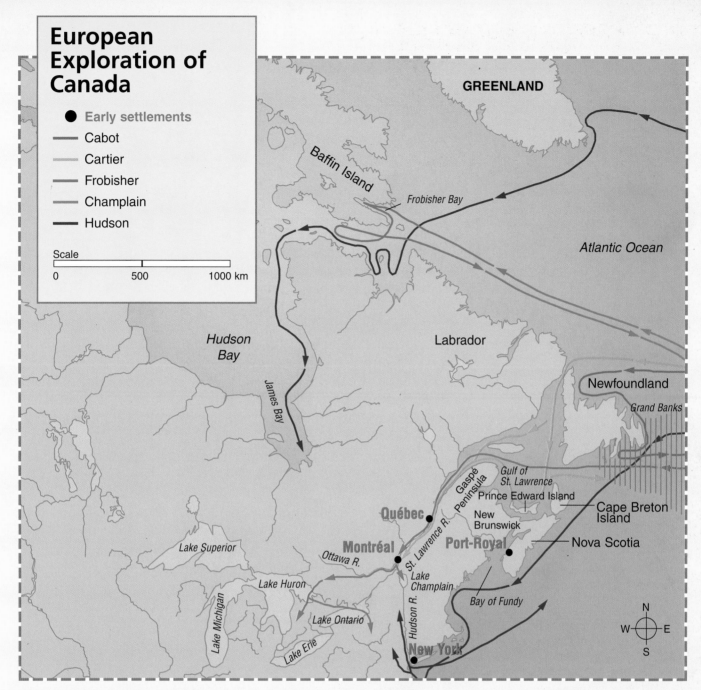

European Exploration of Canada

- ● **Early settlements**
- ── Cabot
- ── Cartier
- ── Frobisher
- ── Champlain
- ── Hudson

Scale

0   500   1000 km

GREENLAND

Baffin Island

Frobisher Bay

Atlantic Ocean

Hudson Bay

Labrador

James Bay

Newfoundland

Grand Banks

Gaspé Peninsula

Gulf of St. Lawrence

Prince Edward Island

Cape Breton Island

Québec

New Brunswick

Nova Scotia

Lake Superior

Montréal

Ottawa R.

St. Lawrence R.

Port-Royal

Lake Huron

Lake Champlain

Bay of Fundy

Lake Michigan

Lake Ontario

Hudson R.

Lake Erie

New York

N
W   E
S

This map shows the places visited by the early explorers and some of their main routes. Because most of eastern Canada was covered with forests, these explorers travelled mainly by water. They sailed along the east coast and up rivers toward the middle of North America. They also sailed northwest to the Arctic Ocean. Many places in Canada had names that were given to them by Aboriginal Peoples before Europeans came. For example, Québec City now stands on the site of Stadacona, and Montréal on the site of Hochelaga. Some places still have names from Aboriginal languages, such as Ottawa. Often, European explorers named places after themselves. Some places have changed their original names. For example, Montréal was once called Ville-Marie, and Annapolis Royal was once called Port-Royal.

Learning from Maps

Compare the explorer's names in the legend with the names of places on the map. How many places are named after explorers?

John Cabot

Finding Information

The Beothuk were Aboriginal people who lived in Newfoundland. Look at the map on page 13. What was the name of the area in which the Beothuk lived?

John Cabot was one of the first European explorers to come to Canada. He was a sea captain and mapmaker. In 1497, he sailed from England to look for a new route to Asia. Instead he found Canada's east coast.

Cabot's ship, the *Matthew*, was **outfitted** by English merchants. They supplied Cabot and his crew of eighteen men with food and trading supplies.

After sailing across the Atlantic Ocean for fifty days, they sighted land. Cabot explored the coast they found. They saw signs that people lived there. They found fishing nets and **snares** set to trap animals, but they did not meet anyone. Cabot rowed ashore and claimed the land for England.

As the *Matthew* sailed on, the ocean became shallow. The ship was surrounded by fish. The crew scooped up a big basket full of fresh Atlantic cod and had a feast.

Cabot had found a wonderful fishing area that became known as the Grand Banks. The Grand Banks is an area of shallow water southeast of Newfoundland. They stretch for 500 kilometres. The water is between 40 and 200 metres deep.

Cabot returned to England to tell about his trip. The merchants were very pleased to hear about the codfish. They needed more food to sell.

The king of England gave Cabot money to pay for another trip. In 1498, Cabot set sail with five ships and over 200 settlers. They never reached their destination. No one knows what happened to Cabot and the settlers. They were probably lost at sea.

However, the Europeans now knew about the Grand Banks. Sailors began to fish there every summer, sailing back to Europe with a **hold** full of fish.

When Cabot reached Canada, he thought he had reached China. Historians think he may have found Cape Breton Island, Labrador, or Newfoundland.

When explorers reached a new land, they claimed it for their country. To do this, some explorers left a symbol, such as a flag. These symbols showed others who came to the same place that it was already claimed by someone else.

In this painting, Cabot is shown raising the first English flag in North America.

Life Aboard the *Matthew*

Imagine that Cabot has invited you to visit his ship, the *Matthew*, upon his return to England. A young member of the crew leads you around the ship. He tells you about sailing to the Grand Banks. Why were the Grand Banks so important to Europeans?

Welcome aboard! My name is Matthew, just like our ship. I'm thirteen years old, the youngest in the crew. I help the caulkers. Wooden ships always leak. Caulkers are people who patch the holes so the ship doesn't fill with water and sink. We also pump out the water that collects in the **bilge** at the bottom of the ship.

We have just returned from a long voyage across the Atlantic Ocean. We were looking for a route to China but instead we found a new land! As we sailed along the coast, we found a place where the sea was filled with fish. We fished and fished, and ate and ate.

The food on the *Matthew* was pretty bad by that time anyway. We only took food with us that would keep for a long time. Most was salted or dried. We took salted fish, meat pickled in salt water, dried peas and beans, onions, cheese, rice, and hard, flat biscuits. Even these foods weren't very good by the end of the trip. The meat was rotten and the dry biscuits had bugs in them. We were very happy to find the codfish.

On our voyage, we all took turns cooking on the deck. We had to be very careful not to set the ship on fire with flying sparks from the cooking fire. When the sea was rough, the ship tossed about, and we couldn't cook at all.

Everyone except the officers slept on the deck in nice weather. When it stormed, we slept in the hold, on top of the cargo. My spot was on top of the onions. After I slept there, I smelled terrible until the rain washed me and my clothes.

Cabot sailed to the Grand Banks. The ocean was full of Atlantic cod. News of the fishing grounds was welcomed in Europe. Fish were an important source of food.

Jacques Cartier

After Cabot's voyage, people came from European countries every year to fish for cod in the Grand Banks. Other Europeans still wanted to find a new route to Asia. Some explorers tried to sail northwest around the new land. Others tried to find a route through it.

Jacques Cartier was a master sailor from St. Malo, France. He had been on fishing trips to the Grand Banks. The French king hired him to search for gold and jewels in the new lands across the Atlantic Ocean and to try to find the Northwest Passage.

Cartier made three voyages of exploration. He left France for his first voyage on April 30, 1534. He had two ships and a crew of sixty-one. It took Cartier twenty days to sail to Newfoundland. He sailed around the north end of the island, down the west side, and into the Gulf of St. Lawrence.

Cartier and his crew spent the summer exploring the Gulf of St. Lawrence, looking for a route to Asia. In June, he discovered Prince Edward Island. He also visited several large bays on the coast of New Brunswick, thinking one of them might be the Northwest Passage.

In July, Cartier landed on the Gaspé Peninsula. Cartier raised a large cross on the shore, claiming this land for France. He met a group of Iroquois who had come to fish on the coast.

Cartier kept a journal in which he recorded what he saw on his voyages. In this journal entry, he described the first group of Aboriginal Peoples he met. They were Beothuk who were fishing and hunting seals along the coast of Newfoundland.

This painting shows Cartier landing on the Gaspé Peninsula in 1534. He met a group of Iroquois who were there fishing.

What do you think?

What do you think the Iroquois thought of Cartier and his crew?

Their chief was named Donnacona. With him were his two sons, Taignoagny and Domagaya. Cartier gave Donnacona gifts of knives, glass beads, combs, and tin rings. In return, the Iroquois shared their food with the Europeans. They gave the visitors fresh fish. They also showed the Europeans how to cook the dried corn, fruits, and nuts they had brought with them from their village, Stadacona. Stadacona was at the same place Québec City is today.

When Cartier returned to France for the winter, he captured Donnacona's sons to take with him. He arrived back in St. Malo, France on September 4, 1534.

After a winter in France, Cartier sailed back to Canada, in 1535. This time he had three ships and a crew of 110 people. When the ships had crossed the ocean, Domagaya and Taignoagny showed Cartier the route up the St. Lawrence River to their home. They arrived in Stadacona in September, 1535.

Cartier explored farther up the river past Stadacona. He found a second group of Aboriginal Peoples living at Hochelaga, on the island of Montréal. Cartier climbed a hill on the island and named it Mount Royal. He could see that the river stretched a long way, but **rapids** made travel by boat look difficult. Cartier returned to Stadacona. There he built a camp where he spent the winter with his crew. The winter was much colder than it was in France. Many of the French became sick, and twenty-five died over the winter. When Cartier sailed home in the spring, he took Donnacona, his two sons, and several other people with him. The Iroquois never returned to their home. Donnacona and the others all died in France.

In 1541, Cartier made his third and last voyage. He left France in May with five ships and a large group of 1 500 people. He wanted to start a settlement on the St. Lawrence River. Cartier and the settlers reached Stadacona in August.

The people of Stadacona were not happy to see Cartier return. He had used land near their homes without talking to them about it first. When he visited Hochelaga on his last visit, he had done so against their wishes. He had not brought Donnacona and the others back from France. At first, Cartier told the people of Stadacona that Donnacona was living in France. Later, he admitted that Donnacona had died.

Cartier spent another winter at a camp on the St. Lawrence River. The winter was hard for the settlers and many died. He sailed home in June 1542. He took some rocks back to France that he thought contained gold and diamonds.

The rocks turned out to be worthless. Cartier's plan to start a settlement had failed. More than sixty years passed before French explorers came to this area again.

July 7, 1534

Nine canoes came to our ship. We rowed out to meet them in two longboats. They made signs to show they wanted to trade. They held up some furs. We sent two men on shore with knives, iron goods, and a red cap for their chief. Before long, they brought their furs over. We soon traded for all the furs they had.

On his first voyage, Cartier met a group of Mi'kmaq people at their summer fishing camp. The Mi'kmaq made signals to show Cartier they wanted to trade with him.

Finding Information

One of the reasons Cartier's settlement failed was that the people of Stadacona no longer wanted to help Cartier. Why did their feelings change?

When Cartier Came to Our Land

Taignoagny was one of Donnacona's sons. He met Cartier on the Gaspé Peninsula in the summer of 1534. This is how Taignoagny could have described his meeting with the newcomers, and the first winter Cartier spent at Stadacona. How did Taignoagny and his people help Cartier?

The newcomers built a tall wooden cross and placed it near the water. My father took me, my brother Domagaya, and several others in our canoes to see the cross. We were careful not to get too close to the ships. We could see many people standing on the decks.

Father stood up in our canoe. He pointed to the cross and gave a long speech to the newcomers. Then he pointed to the land all around us. He wanted the newcomers to know that the Creator had given the land for all of us to use. The newcomers should have asked him, the chief, if they could use the land too.

Their leader was named Jacques Cartier. He held up an axe. He pretended he wanted to trade the axe for Father's black bearskin robe. When our canoe drew near the ship, some of Cartier's men jumped in. They grabbed us and pulled us on board. They told us with signs that the cross was just a **landmark** to guide them back to the spot, but I didn't believe them.

Cartier gave my brother and me cloth shirts, bright ribbons, and red caps. He put shiny chains around our necks. He gave Father and the others axes and knives. My brother and I stayed on the ship while everyone else went back to shore in the canoes.

At noon the next day, Father returned with some of our people. They brought lots of fish. Father asked Cartier to let us go, but he refused.

The next day, Cartier's ships sailed away. He took us with him. After many days at sea, we landed in Cartier's country. It was called France. We saw many interesting things there.

We learned to speak Cartier's language. Everyone we met asked us about our land. "How big is it?" and "Does it have any gold?" they asked.

Domagaya and I told them what they wanted to hear, because we wanted to go home as quickly as possible. Our answers made many of them eager to see our homeland.

After winter passed, Cartier set sail again with three ships. This time, we helped him find his way back. We guided him to the great river that flowed by our village.

When we reached our home at Stadacona, our people greeted us joyfully. Father thanked Cartier for bringing us back safely.

Cartier found a good **harbour** for his ships not far from our village. He told us he wanted to go farther up the river. He asked us to go with him. Father did not want Cartier to go upriver to Hochelaga until he reached a trading agreement with our people. Cartier went anyway. He took about fifty sailors with him. The rest of his crew stayed behind. They began to build a fort near our village, even though they had not asked us whether they could.

When Cartier came back, he told us he had gone as far as the village of Hochelaga. The people he met at Hochelaga had given him a warm welcome. They brought him fish and corn bread. They invited him to a feast, but he wanted to get back to Stadacona before winter set in and the river froze.

That winter, Cartier's men became sick. Their arms and legs swelled. Their gums hurt and their teeth became loose. They had a **disease** called **scurvy**. Many of them died.

Cartier asked us to help him cure his men. Domagaya told Cartier how to make tea from the bark and needles of white cedar trees.

Two women from our village went to help Cartier gather some cedar branches. They showed him how to grind the bark and the needles, and how to boil them in water. When the sick people drank the cedar drink, they began to get better. Soon they had their health and strength back.

When spring came, Cartier got ready to sail away. Father, Domagaya, and I went down to Cartier's fort to say goodbye. Cartier invited us inside, but then he deceived us. He made us and several other people from Stadacona get onto his ship. He made us sail to France with him again.

This painting shows the Iroquois helping Cartier make a cure for scurvy from the branches of cedar trees.

Martin Frobisher

Martin Frobisher was an English explorer who thought he could reach Asia by sailing northwest around North America. Queen Elizabeth I of England ordered some merchants to help supply his ships for the journey.

Frobisher was among the first European explorers of the Arctic. He sailed as far as Baffin Island looking for the Northwest Passage.

Frobisher made his first trip in the summer of 1576. He explored the coast of Labrador. Then he sailed farther north. He discovered a bay near a large island, which was later named Baffin Island after William Baffin, a later explorer. At first, Frobisher thought the bay might be the Northwest Passage. He named it Frobisher Bay, after himself.

One of Frobisher's crew went ashore with gifts for the Inuit who lived along the coast. The **Inuit** visited Frobisher's ship to trade their sealskin and bearskin coats for bells, mirrors, and other small articles. Using sign language, Frobisher asked one of them to guide his ship through the passage. The **Inuk** agreed. Five sailors went with him to get his **kayak** so he could guide them. Frobisher never saw these men again.

Before Frobisher returned to England, he captured an Inuk man in his kayak. He also took back some rock he had found on the shore. He thought it contained gold. Frobisher was eager to get back to the area where there was more of this rock. Merchants agreed to pay for another voyage.

On his second voyage in 1577, Frobisher and his crew collected tonnes of the rock. Frobisher also tried to find out what had happened to the five sailors who had disappeared.

While some of Frobisher's crew were searching for gold, they met a group of Inuit and exchanged gifts with them. One day, when Frobisher and his crew started to leave, the Inuit followed. Frobisher tried to capture two of them, because he thought they might know something about his missing crew. When the Inuit defended themselves, one of their arrows wounded Frobisher. The fight ended when Frobisher's crew captured one of the Inuit men.

Frobisher did not give up looking for his missing crew. One day, when he found an empty tent, he thought it might have belonged to his men. His crew tried to catch a group of Inuit to ask about the tent. When the Inuit escaped in their kayaks, the English rowed after them, firing their guns. The Inuit landed and defended themselves from shore.

A fierce battle took place. The Inuit fought bravely, but their arrows were no match for the English guns. A few of the Inuit were killed. The English also captured two women. One of them had a small child. The English let the older woman go, but took the mother and baby back to England. They also took the Inuk man they had captured earlier. All three became ill and died in England.

In 1578, Frobisher made his third voyage. This time he had fifteen ships. The ships were blown off course by storms but they landed on an island. Again, Frobisher hauled tonnes of rock back to England. There he got some bad news. The rock was worthless. It contained no gold at all. It was iron pyrite, known as fool's gold.

Frobisher was discouraged. He decided to stop exploring. He joined Queen Elizabeth's navy, and later on, she made him Sir Martin Frobisher.

Frobisher never found out what happened to the five missing sailors. Three hundred years later, an American explorer heard an Inuit story about five Europeans who had come with the first ships. These men lived with the Inuit for a few years. Then they built a large boat and sailed out into the open water. They were never seen again.

What do you think?

1. How did Frobisher's actions affect his relations with the Inuit?

2. What ideas about the Inuit do you think Europeans would get by looking at the painting on this page?

On Frobisher's second voyage in 1577, he took an artist named John White with him. White painted this scene showing a fight between the Inuit and the English.

Samuel de Champlain

Samuel de Champlain was a French explorer and mapmaker. He was also one of the first European people to set up trading posts and settlements in early Canada. Champlain made many of the first drawings and maps of the new land. He wrote descriptions of the people he met on his travels, and of the places he explored around the St. Lawrence River. Champlain made his first trip to Canada in 1603. He came with people who planned to start a fur-trading post in the new land. As Cartier had done, they sailed up the St. Lawrence River, but they decided not to stay there. Instead, they sailed back to the Atlantic coast where they built a settlement called Port-Royal on the Bay of Fundy.

Champlain explored the coast in that area, but he was more interested in the St. Lawrence. In 1608, he sailed up the great river again. He decided to stop at a spot along the river protected by cliffs. He started a fur-trading post at this spot.

He named it Québec because the Aboriginal Peoples had called it *kebec*. This word means "where the river gets narrow." There was good soil nearby, so farms could be started to grow food for the traders. Québec was also close to a rich supply of furs. Furs were needed to pay for the upkeep of the settlement and for Champlain's explorations.

Champlain began to make friends with the Algonquin and Montagnais people who lived nearby. Champlain wanted them to bring their furs to the trading post at Québec.

Champlain travelled to Georgian Bay by canoe in 1615. He wanted to build better relations between the French and Huron.

What do you think?

How do you think Aboriginal guides might have helped Champlain?

Champlain believed he might find the Northwest Passage in the area around the new settlement. On one trip, he travelled south with a group of Aboriginal Peoples. They went along the Richelieu River until they reached a large lake. Today this lake is called Lake Champlain.

A few years later, Champlain went exploring again. He was looking for a route west to a sea he had heard about from the Aboriginal Peoples. In 1615, he reached Lake Huron, where he met the Huron people. From there he headed southeast and reached Lake Ontario. He was disappointed because neither of these lakes was the Pacific Ocean.

After this trip, Champlain never went exploring again. However, he encouraged some of the young men who had travelled with him to continue exploring. When they returned to Québec, he always talked with them about their explorations. He also talked to Aboriginal Peoples about the lands to the north and west of the St. Lawrence.

Near the end of his life, Champlain used all the information from his trips to draw a map. This map was the first to show the rivers and lakes of eastern Canada in much detail. The map helped other people who explored after Champlain.

Champlain met Huron people at their home on Georgian Bay, part of Lake Huron. The French became fur-trading partners with the Huron. The Huron could get a large supply of furs by trading with their neighbours to the west.

What Should Champlain Do?

Champlain worked with many groups of people while he lived in Canada. Each group of people had different ideas about how Champlain should spend his time. Sometimes the ideas were in conflict.

FRENCH MERCHANT

I gave Champlain money to finance his voyages. I paid for his ships, his crew, and his supplies. The only way I can get my money back is from the sale of furs.

I want Champlain to spend his time trading so he can repay my loan. He can't do that if he is always exploring or if he is back in France looking for more settlers.

QUÉBEC SETTLER

I came to this new land to farm with my husband and children. We moved here because Champlain promised to help us clear the land to grow crops. He said that other settlers would join us, but only a few have come. We want him to keep his promises.

We also need him to build a strong fort at Québec. We are afraid that our settlement might be attacked by the English and the Iroquois. The Iroquois are the allies of the English and the enemies of our Aboriginal trading partners. We need Champlain to defend Québec and help it grow.

FRENCH OFFICIAL

We sent Champlain to North America to search for a route to Asia. We want him to keep exploring until he finds it.

We also want him to help run the settlement he has started. He knows the people and the land better than anyone, so he can act as governor and judge.

We expect that he will send new maps and pictures showing us what he has seen. We want him to write reports about all his activities and send them to us in France.

**Could Champlain satisfy all these people?
What would you have done?**

Henry Hudson

In 1609, another English explorer, Henry Hudson, tried to find the Northwest Passage. Hudson had already tried to sail to Asia by way of the North Pole in 1607. In 1609, he tried a different direction. Hudson and his crew sailed west across the Atlantic Ocean to North America. He sailed his ship, the *Half Moon*, up a river that begins where the city of New York is today. When Hudson realized the river was not the Northwest Passage, he returned to England. Today the river is called the Hudson River.

In April 1610, Hudson and his crew sailed to look for the Northwest Passage again. This time, with Frobisher's maps to help him, Hudson sailed northwest into the Arctic waters. After sailing through a narrow **strait** filled with ice, he entered a large, open body of water. He followed the coast that bordered the water. He thought he had reached the west coast of North America. In fact, he had discovered a bay that was later named Hudson Bay after him.

After months of searching for a way out of the bay, Hudson found his ship, the *Discovery*, blocked by land. Winter was coming. Hudson and his crew landed and spent the winter on the shore near their boat. The weather was terrible. The sailors became ill with scurvy. Food supplies ran low.

In the spring, before the ice melted, an Aboriginal person came to trade with the crew. Hudson and some of the crew went on foot to look for more Aboriginal Peoples, but they met no one.

As soon as the ice had melted and the ship was free to sail, the crew wanted to return home. Hudson would not listen. He decided to continue his search for the Northwest Passage. Finally, the crew **mutinied**, and set Hudson, his son, and some loyal crew members adrift in a small boat. Hudson and the others did not survive.

Although Hudson did not find the Northwest Passage, his explorations later helped England lay a claim to the rich fur-trading area around Hudson Bay. There were now two routes to get furs from Canada to Europe. The French could ship furs to France by way of the St. Lawrence River. The English could ship furs from Hudson Bay to England.

In his attempt to find a northern route between Europe and Asia, Henry Hudson sailed farther north than any earlier explorer.

Finding Information

List some of the problems Hudson had on his voyage.

Mutiny on the *Discovery*

One of the men who sailed with Hudson was his nineteen-year-old son, John. If John had kept a journal of his trip, it might have been similar to the following passage. What does this journal tell you about the hardships explorers faced?

April 17, 1610 We set sail today, heading west. Father is sure we will be the first to reach China using this route.

June 16 Yesterday ice nearly crushed our ship. The ice was so close I could almost touch it. Father wants to keep going even though the men are angry.

July 27 We are away from the ice now. There is open sea and the weather is warm. Father says we are close to China.

July 29 We went by an island with lots of birds on it. The crew wanted to stop to hunt. Father would not stop. He said we would soon find an even better place.

August 29. It's getting colder. The land is rocky and empty.

September 20 Father has decided to stop for the winter. The crew are building a shack for shelter and hunting birds for food. I'm freezing. My coat isn't warm enough. Ice is forming around the ship.

December 8 Many men are sick. The ship's carpenter died yesterday. The crew fought over who would get his coat.

The *Discovery* returned to England, but no one ever found Hudson and the other people set adrift.

March 15, 1611 An Aboriginal man came today. Father gave him a knife, a mirror, and some buttons. The man returned with two deerskins and two beaver skins on his sled. Using signs, he showed he was willing to trade one beaver skin for a knife, and one beaver skin for a mirror and buttons. He traded the two deerskins for one axe.

June 18 Hooray! Our ship is finally free from the ice. We are almost ready to set sail.

June 20 I heard the men grumbling last night. They think Father is hiding food from them. They no longer want to explore.

June 23 The crew took over the *Discovery* today. They ordered Father, me, and some other crew members to get into the small boat. Then they sailed away. What will happen to us?

In Summary

1. While they were looking for a shorter route to Asia, European explorers found a new land.

2. The early explorers travelled in eastern Canada and the St. Lawrence River valley. Some tried to sail northwest through the Arctic Ocean. The explorers soon discovered that the new land had rich resources of fish and furs.

3. The explorers met Aboriginal Peoples in the new land they visited. The explorers began to trade with them. Sometimes the explorers also fought with them.

4. Cabot first visited the Grand Banks near Newfoundland in 1497. Europeans began fishing there every summer.

5. Cartier sailed to Canada from France in 1534. He explored part of the east coast and sailed up the St. Lawrence River. The Aboriginal Peoples he met taught Cartier many things about the new land.

6. Frobisher began European exploration of the Arctic. He reached Baffin Island, where he met some Inuit people.

7. Champlain explored the east coast and the land along the St. Lawrence River. He helped start French settlements in the new land. He traded furs with the Aboriginal Peoples.

8. Hudson discovered an important route into the middle of North America that would help fur traders. The Hudson Bay area became important to the English fur trade.

9. The explorers reported their discoveries in the new land in many ways. Often they drew maps and pictures of what they had seen. Sometimes they captured Aboriginal Peoples to take back to Europe with them. The reports encouraged other Europeans to travel to North America.

Reliving the Past

1. On foot, explore an area near you. You could explore a park, a valley, or a farm. Carry a notebook with you. During your trip, stop about once every five minutes to record your experiences. Write about what you have seen, how far you have come, and any problems you have had. After the trip, compare your journal with those of other students. Did you record the same information? How could this exercise help you understand the journals left by explorers?

2. Role play a meeting between an Iroquois youth and a European of the same age. How would you show that you were friendly? Is giving presents a good way to make friends? Why or why not? What kinds of questions would you ask each other?

Part Three

Fur Traders

Shortly after Europeans began sailing to Canada to explore and to fish, they found out that Canada was a land with many fur-bearing animals. When explorers and fishers began trading with Aboriginal Peoples for fresh food, they learned that the Aboriginal Peoples had furs from the animals they hunted. The fur trade in Canada began because many Europeans wanted these furs. Both the French and the English used furs, especially beaver fur, to make hats and to trim other clothing. They became partners in the fur trade with the Aboriginal Peoples.

The French built trading posts on the St. Lawrence River and traded with Aboriginal Peoples who came to their posts with furs. Later on, the French travelled west to find more furs.

The English traded with the Aboriginal Peoples of Newfoundland and on the Atlantic coast south of the French settlements. The English formed the Hudson's Bay Company in 1670 and built trading posts around Hudson Bay.

The French and English competed with each other to get more furs from the Aboriginal Peoples. The fur trade caused many changes in the lives of the Europeans and the Aboriginal Peoples.

The fur traders continued the exploration of Canada as they travelled to new areas to find more fur. The Aboriginal Peoples they met helped them survive in the new areas.

Beaver fur from Canada was of high quality. Canada's cold winters made the fur grow long and thick. The picture to the left shows a trapper with his furs. Round beaver pelts are shown at the front of the photo.

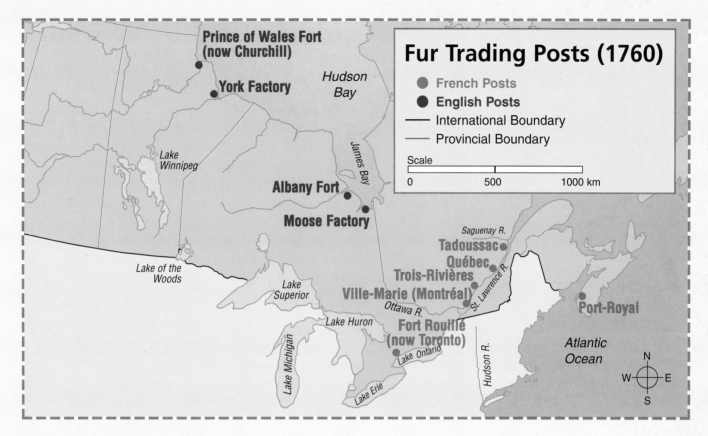

Fur Trading Posts (1760)

- (grey dot) French Posts
- (black dot) English Posts
- International Boundary
- Provincial Boundary

Scale
0   500   1000 km

Prince of Wales Fort (now Churchill)

York Factory

Hudson Bay

Lake Winnipeg

James Bay

Albany Fort

Moose Factory

Lake of the Woods

Lake Superior

Saguenay R.

Tadoussac

Québec

Trois-Rivières

Ville-Marie (Montréal)

St. Lawrence R.

Port-Royal

Ottawa R.

Fort Rouillé (now Toronto)

Lake Huron

Lake Michigan

Lake Ontario

Hudson R.

Atlantic Ocean

Lake Erie

N W E S

At first, the Europeans only traded with the Aboriginal Peoples in the summer. Then they sailed home to Europe for the winter. As the fur trade grew, some traders and merchants decided to live in the new land so they could trade for furs all year round. The furs were collected at the trading posts and were then taken to Europe and sold. This map shows some of the most important trading posts around 1760.

The Europeans wanted beaver fur to make hats. Beaver hats for men became fashionable in the 1600s, but there were not very many beavers left in Europe by then. Shown here are some of the different kinds of beaver hats people wore.

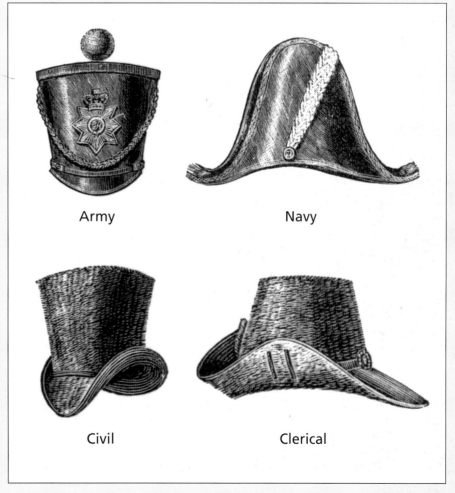

Army

Navy

Civil

Clerical

The Beginning of the Fur Trade

The fur trade in Canada began slowly. At first, Europeans thought the new land was only a good source of fish. Many European fishers arrived each summer to fish the Grand Banks. Some of them also sailed up the St. Lawrence River to fish.

Fishers met Aboriginal Peoples who lived near the ocean. They began to trade metal and cloth goods for furs and fresh meat. Explorers also met Aboriginal Peoples on their voyages. As Cartier sailed past the coast of New Brunswick in 1534, he met Mi'kmaq people who were eager to trade with him.

The Aboriginal Peoples liked the goods from Europe. More and more of them began to travel to the coast and the St. Lawrence River each summer to trade. They traded their furs for knives, axes, pots, and other goods.

The Europeans began to realize that great wealth could be made by selling furs from Canada. Furs from Canada were easy to sell in Europe.

Ships began sailing to Canada just to trade for furs. Some fishers stopped fishing and became fur traders instead. The French traders began sailing farther up the St. Lawrence River, looking for Aboriginal people with furs to trade. The French claimed this area for France, so only they could trade for the furs in the region. The English claimed Newfoundland and the Atlantic coast of what is now the United States.

Before the Europeans came, many Aboriginal Peoples met in the summer to trade with one another where the Saguenay River meets the St. Lawrence. They called this spot Tadoussac. European fishing crews began to go there too. They hunted whales and fished. They began to trade knives, axes, and pots for the furs Aboriginal Peoples brought to trade.

A Montagnais Visits Tadoussac

The Montagnais people began trading with Europeans at Tadoussac around 1600. This story tells what it might have been like when the Aboriginal Peoples started trading with European traders. What changes did the fur trade bring to Aboriginal Peoples' lives?

Winter was very fine this year. About forty of my people hunted together all winter. In the spring, we travelled to our summer camp. Most of the band was already there, so we soon set out for the large meeting place on the coast where we usually spent the summer. On the coast, there were many Naskapi people from the north, and there were Cree and Algonquin people from the east, as well as many of our Montagnais. As usual, we had a good time talking and playing games. The weather had been good, and most people were healthy and had many things to trade.

My mother wanted to find some metal knives. She had heard that there were **foreigners** on the coast with knives to trade. Some Algonquin people heard us talking, and they showed us some metal goods they had. They wanted to trade with us, but would only take beaver skins. We didn't have many skins. Beavers aren't that useful to us—not like caribou.

Some other families said that Tadoussac, the meeting place by the two rivers, was now a year-round trading place. There were foreigners there, they said, with many trading goods. The Algonquin traders were angry because they wanted us to trade with them. My father just laughed. We would get busy trapping beavers, he said, and then take a trip to Tadoussac ourselves.

All the adults in our group agreed this would be a good idea. We set off to the southeast, stopping to trap beavers along the way.

As we got closer to Tadoussac, we met more and more people who wanted to trade goods for our beaver skins.

When we arrived at Tadoussac, there were people everywhere. We saw many foreigners wearing strange clothes. To our surprise, we even saw a group of Montagnais people wearing foreign clothes! There were more people and more trading goods than we had ever imagined.

We looked around until we met another group of Montagnais people. They invited us to build our shelter near them. We all had supper together, sharing our caribou and dried fish and their strange, foreign food. We were surprised to learn that they no longer hunted caribou in the woods all winter. Instead, they went trapping far into the northwest in the winter and spent all summer at Tadoussac. They didn't hunt caribou or fish anymore. They only hunted beavers. "The beaver does everything perfectly well," joked one of their leaders. "It makes kettles, axes, knives, and bread. It makes everything."

"They are very clever," said my father thoughtfully.

"Yes, and you're too old to change," my mother told him. "Let's go back to our old hunting grounds in the woods. Our children will grow clever enough to have the beaver do all their work for them."

Everyone laughed, but I knew we would go back to hunt the caribou, as my mother had said. I wondered whether we would come back to trade for foreign goods at Tadoussac next summer.

The drawing above shows a Huron person wearing wooden armour. The drawing below shows an Iroquois man ready for battle.

The First Trading Posts

The fur trade grew. Merchants in France started companies to collect the furs in Canada. In 1600, one of the French companies built a trading post at Tadoussac so it could trade there all year. The post did not last very long. The French did not know how to survive the cold, snowy Canadian winters.

In 1605, the French tried again to build a lasting trading post. Champlain started a trading-post settlement on the east coast. It was a little warmer there, and there were fewer traders competing for furs. Sixty French settlers went to the new post at Port-Royal, on the Bay of Fundy. Port-Royal was the first French settlement in **Acadia**. Acadia included Nova Scotia, New Brunswick, Prince Edward Island, and the Gaspé Peninsula.

The French settlers met the Mi'kmaq people who lived nearby. The French traded for furs with the Mi'kmaq and became their friends, but the furs from the Mi'kmaq were not enough to pay for the settlement at Port-Royal.

In 1608, the French tried another spot for their trading post. This time Champlain chose the spot where Stadacona had once stood, at Québec. Later on, the French built other trading posts along the St. Lawrence River.

The St. Lawrence valley was a good place for the fur traders. It was close to a rich supply of furs. Many rivers in the valley went inland. The French could easily ship the furs brought from the Aboriginal Peoples back to France.

Many Aboriginal Peoples who lived near the St. Lawrence valley, such as the Huron and Algonquin, became the trading partners of the French. South of the Great Lakes lived the Iroquois, a group of five Aboriginal Peoples who had joined together. The Iroquois became trading partners of the English traders on the Hudson River.

As the fur trade grew, the Iroquois wanted to trade more furs with their English partners. There were no longer many furs in the Iroquois and Huron lands. Both groups wanted to trade for furs with other Aboriginal groups farther west, but the Huron controlled the water-routes to the West.

During the 1600s, the Iroquois fought with the French-Huron trading partnership for control over the sources of furs. The Iroquois sent war parties armed with English guns to the St. Lawrence valley to try to drive the French away. They attacked Huronia to stop the Huron from blocking the trade routes. By 1650, many Huron had been killed. The rest fled to live with other Aboriginal groups. In 1690, the Iroquois were defeated by the French and the Iroquois Wars ended.

What do you think?

1. How would wooden armor have protected the Huron?

2. Why might a French artist draw a fierce-looking Iroquois?

Making Choices

Adam Dollard: An Unselfish Hero?

The French and their friends, the Huron and Algonquin, fought the Iroquois many times. They raided each other's lands. They tried to take each other's furs. During the 1600s, French settlements along the St. Lawrence were sometimes attacked by the Iroquois.

The story of Adam Dollard's battle with the Iroquois at the Long Sault, a series of rapids on the Ottawa River, has been told many times. In some older history books, Dollard is called a hero. In newer books, his reasons for fighting the Iroquois have been questioned. Here are different versions of his story.

THE BASIC FACTS

Adam Dollard des Ormeaux was a young French soldier. In the spring of 1660, Dollard and seventeen friends travelled up the Ottawa River. A small group of Huron and Algonquin people joined them. They all camped near the rapids called the Long Sault.

The next day, a large fleet of Iroquois canoes came down the river. Shots were fired. A battle raged for seven days. At the end, Dollard and all his friends were dead.

QUÉBEC SETTLER

A rumour reached Montréal. An Iroquois force was spending the winter up the Ottawa River. It was part of an Iroquois army that planned to destroy Montréal.

Dollard and his friends decided to strike first. They met the Iroquois at the Long Sault. For seven days, the French and Huron battled the Iroquois from an old Huron fort. Finally, their food, water, and gunpowder ran out.

The bravery of the French impressed the Iroquois. They gave up their plans to attack Montréal and went home.

NEW VERSION

Dollard knew that small groups of Iroquois came down the Ottawa River each spring. Their canoes would be full of furs from the north. He hoped to surprise the Iroquois and take their furs.

Dollard's group hid in an old Huron fort near the Long Sault. Instead of traders, a party of Iroquois warriors came down the river. They trapped Dollard and his friends in the fort.

After a long battle, the French lit their last powder keg. It fell back and exploded among them, killing them all.

Compare the two versions of the story. Make a chart that
lists at least four differences between them.
Why might there be different versions of the same event?
Which version do you think is correct?
What other facts might you need to decide whether Dollard
was a hero?

Radisson and Groseilliers

Pierre Radisson and his brother-in-law, Médard Chouart de Groseilliers, were fur traders from Trois-Rivières. They explored the area north of the Great Lakes, looking for furs. The Aboriginal Peoples they met told them there were plenty of beavers farther north, toward Hudson Bay.

The partners travelled north and returned from their explorations with sixty canoes filled with furs. They expected a warm welcome. However, the officials at Québec thought too many young men were leaving the settlement to live and trade with the Aboriginal Peoples. They had decided that no one could trade furs without a licence. Since Radisson and Groseilliers had no trading licences, they were fined and their furs were taken away. Groseilliers went to jail for a time.

Radisson and Groseilliers were angry. They sailed to England, where the king agreed to let them trade for furs around Hudson Bay. In June 1668, they set off in two ships. Storms forced Radisson's ship to return to England, but Groseillier's ship kept going. That year, Groseilliers built a small trading post on Hudson Bay. In the spring, he and his crew traded with a large group of Aboriginal people. When Groseilliers' ship returned to England, it carried a large cargo of furs.

The English merchants were delighted with the rich furs. In 1670, they started the Hudson's Bay Company. The king granted it the right to trade for furs in all the lands drained by rivers flowing into Hudson Bay.

There were now three important fur-trading areas in North America. The English traded on Hudson Bay and on the Hudson River farther south. The French traded along the St. Lawrence River and near the Great Lakes.

Iroquois attacks made it difficult for the Huron to take their furs to the trading posts on the St. Lawrence River. As a result, some young French traders went to live and trade with the Aboriginal Peoples, and bring the furs back to the French trading posts themselves. They were called **coureurs de bois**, which means "runners of the woods." They learned many skills from the Aboriginal Peoples. This painting shows coureurs de bois canoeing through some rapids.

The Hudson's Bay Company

The English who worked for the Hudson's Bay Company built trading posts on the shores of Hudson Bay. They were called factories because the person in charge was called a chief factor. The factories were built where rivers flowed into the bay, so it was easy for Aboriginal Peoples to bring their furs to the posts.

Many people worked at the company factories. The chief factor, the clerk, and sometimes a junior clerk did the trading. Other people, such as doctors, carpenters, and tailors, also lived at the posts.

The English and the French had different ways of trading with the Aboriginal Peoples. Instead of travelling to trade with them as the French did, the English company traders stayed in their trading posts. They waited for the Aboriginal Peoples to bring their furs to the posts.

The English fur traders did not try to build lasting settlements as the French did. The English who came to Hudson Bay were interested only in trading for furs. The French and the English competed with each other for furs from the Aboriginal Peoples.

Peter Rindisbacher painted this picture of York Factory. It was the most important Hudson's Bay Company trading post for many years. It controlled the rivers leading to the west.

Hudson's Bay Company Price List

Trade Goods	Cost
1 gun	14 beaver pelts
5 pounds (2.2 kg) gunpowder	1 beaver pelt
1 hatchet	1 beaver pelt
1 yard (1 m) cloth	3 beaver pelts
1 pound (0.5 kg) tobacco	2 beaver pelts
4 knives	1 beaver pelt
1 kettle	1 1/2 beaver pelts
1 large roll of string	1 1/4 beaver pelts

This chart shows the number of beaver pelts the Hudson's Bay Company charged for certain trade goods in 1720.

Finding Information

1. Which of these goods cost the most?

2. How might the prices of these trade goods have been set?

3. How might these goods have changed Aboriginal ways of life?

A Cree Boy Visits York Factory

This story is told by an eleven-year-old Cree boy who went with his father on a trip to York Factory to trade furs for English goods. How does he describe the trading ceremony at the post?

I could smell the sea and knew we must be close to the English trading post. We had been paddling our canoes, loaded with furs, for many days. We were glad to arrive.

When we could see the post, we shouted and fired our guns as a greeting. A loud boom from the post made me shake. Father explained that the people at the post had returned our greeting with a shot from their cannon.

We landed and set up camp just outside the trading post. I looked for children my own age, but there were none.

I was proud that my father was chosen to lead this trading voyage. I watched as he met the English leader, who was called the chief factor.

Father and the chief factor smoked a **peace pipe** together for about an hour. Sharing the peace pipe showed the friendship that would exist between them. Then Father and the chief factor took turns giving speeches. Father described our canoes and our furs. The chief factor told us why the English would always be our friends.

The chief factor gave Father a fine set of clothing and other gifts. The rest of us got gifts too. The men got tobacco. I was given a long hunting knife.

The next day, Father gave gifts of beaver pelts to the English. He made another speech. He told the chief factor how far we had come, and he asked the English to trade fairly with us. We sat in a circle and the men smoked the peace pipe again.

The chief factor then took us to the store room of the trading post. Only Father went inside. The rest of us stayed in the trading room. We presented our furs through a window in the wall. Then we chose knives, kettles, cloth, and guns in return for our furs. Father made sure that everything went smoothly during the trade.

The chief factor said goodbye. He invited us to come back next year to trade our furs. After loading our canoes with all the goods we had received for our furs, we started the long trip home.

This painting by artist Peter Rindisbacher shows a Cree hunting family arriving at York Factory.

Henry Kelsey

Henry Kelsey joined the Hudson's Bay Company as a clerk when he was only seventeen years old. He went to York Factory to work at the trading post. Kelsey worked for the company for forty years. The Cree who came to trade their furs at York Factory became Kelsey's friends. He learned to speak their language and made several trips with them along the coast of Hudson Bay.

In 1690, the Hudson's Bay Company sent Kelsey south on a trip. He was sent to invite the Assiniboine people to trade at Hudson Bay. He travelled with a group of Cree returning to their homeland toward the southwest. On the long journey by canoe, the men and women in the group shared the work.

When Kelsey reached the prairie grasslands, he left his Cree guides and went farther west to find the Assiniboine. He met the Assiniboine and spent two years hunting with them before returning home to York Factory. Kelsey had opened up a new trading area for the Hudson's Bay Company.

What do you think?

How might the way of life of a plains people be different from the way of life of a forest people?

Kelsey was the first European to see the bison. Later on, the bison became an important source of food and hides for the traders.

Aboriginal Women in the Fur Trade

Aboriginal women played an important role in the fur trade. Without their skills and hard work, the fur trade would not have been possible. Many of the fur traders married Aboriginal women. These women did a lot of the work at the posts.

Aboriginal women often went on fur-trading trips with their husbands. Many acted as guides. They worked with the men to paddle the canoes and carried heavy loads across **portages**. They set up camp when they stopped, and prepared meals.

Aboriginal women had many skills important to the fur traders. They prepared food such as **pemmican**. Pemmican is light to carry and keeps a long time without spoiling. Aboriginal women also knew how to make medicines from plants.

Women made or helped make many items of value. They made blankets and clothing, including moccasins. They helped make snowshoes. The men made the frames of snowshoes and the women made the webbing for them. They gathered and split spruce roots used to make birchbark canoes. They also collected spruce gum, which was used to make the canoes waterproof.

Sometimes Aboriginal women trapped smaller animals for meat and fur. The women were skilled at cleaning and preparing pelts and hides.

The fur traders learned many skills from their Aboriginal wives. They learned the languages and customs of their wives' people. If a woman from an Aboriginal group married a trader, she often acted as an interpreter and peacemaker among her people and the traders. The women helped their husbands communicate with Aboriginal Peoples. This improved their trading relationships.

Finding Information

Why was pemmican useful to fur traders?

In this picture, a woman pounds meat to make pemmican. Pemmican is a food made from strips of lean meat that are dried, pounded, and mixed with melted fat. Sometimes crushed wild berries are added for extra flavour.

Thanadelthur: Guide and Peacemaker

Thanadelthur was a Dene (Chipewyan) woman from the lands west of Hudson Bay. She helped expand the fur trade north and west of Hudson Bay. Before she died in 1717, she might have described her life in the following way. What skills made her a good guide? What skills helped her succeed as a peacemaker?

The fur trade brought many changes to the lives of my people. We began to compete with the Cree people who came into our territory looking for furs.

One spring, a group of Cree attacked our camp. My cousin and I were captured. A year later, we managed to escape. We hid in the forest and trapped small animals for food. Then the weather turned cold and my cousin died.

This picture by Franklin Arbuckle shows Thanadelthur helping to make peace between the Dene and the Cree.

I followed some tracks that led to the goose-hunting camp of some English traders from Hudson Bay. They took me to a trading post called York Factory.

I lived there over the winter and learned to speak English. I told the chief factor about my people and the rich furs in my homeland. He listened carefully to my stories. He told me that he wanted my people to bring their furs to the Hudson's Bay Company posts. He asked me if I knew how to make peace between the Dene and the Cree.

I thought about the problem. I offered to lead a peace mission to my people. The English factor agreed. In the spring, about 150 of us left York Factory. Most of our group were Cree who lived near the post.

Our long journey was not easy. Illness forced us to split up. Most people returned to York Factory. Only a few of us made it to the Cree camp.

That is when I took over. I told the Cree that in ten days I would find my people and bring them to make peace. I left our camp and set off alone for Dene lands. I found a large band of my people a few days later. I talked and talked to get them to believe the Cree wanted to make peace. They finally agreed to come with me.

On the tenth day, we reached the Cree camp. Then I had to persuade the Cree to agree to peace. Finally, both sides smoked a peace pipe. Ten of our people went to York Factory to become traders and interpreters. One of them was my brother. We planned to return to our people in the spring.

It has been a cold winter. I am very ill. I think I may never see my people again.

Pierre de La Vérendrye

The Hudson's Bay Company controlled the fur trade northwest of the Great Lakes. The French also wanted to trade for furs farther west because there were not many furs left in the Great Lakes area. In 1731, a French trader and explorer named Pierre de La Vérendrye set out from a French trading post on Lake Superior. With him were his sons and his nephew. Aboriginal Peoples helped the French traders find their way.

They travelled toward the fur country in the West. It was a hard route, with many portages. On their journey, the traders built new fur-trading posts for the French. In 1732, La Vérendrye reached Lake of the Woods, where he built a large post. In 1734, La Vérendrye and his family reached a spot near Lake Winnipeg, where they built a trading post called Fort Maurepas. They continued west to explore the Prairies and build new trading posts. They found that the Saskatchewan River was the best route west to lands where the furs were good.

La Vérendrye and his family worked hard to trade with the Aboriginal Peoples they met. They told the Aboriginal Peoples that it was better and easier for them to trade with the French than with the English at their posts on Hudson Bay.

When La Vérendrye travelled through the area now known as Manitoba, he met some Cree people who had moved westward onto the Prairies because of the fur trade. Later, many other Aboriginal Peoples moved westward to find more furs to supply the Europeans. The Cree and the Assiniboine traded with Aboriginal Peoples farther west and with the Hudson's Bay Company trading posts. After the Europeans moved to the plains themselves, the Aboriginal Peoples continued to supply the Europeans with pemmican and bison hides.

People with Different Ideas

This is how two traders, one from the St. Lawrence River valley and one from the Hudson's Bay Company, might each have tried to persuade an Aboriginal chief to trade with him.

FRENCH TRADER

Why do you trade with the English? You must carry your furs long distances to their trading posts on Hudson Bay. If they don't want all your furs, you must carry them back to your homes. The English won't even let you into their storehouse to see the goods they have to trade.

You should trade with us. We accept all your pelts. We even travel to your homes to buy them. We give you supplies and don't ask for payment until you have next year's pelts.

HUDSON BAY TRADER

Why do you trade with the French? Their trade goods aren't as good as ours. Their tobacco tastes like sawdust. They cause trouble in your groups.

You should trade with us. Our goods are less expensive. It is worth making the trip to our post to get a fair price for your furs. If you don't want to travel so far, you may trade your furs with the Cree or the Assiniboine. They will bring the furs to us.

This sketch shows a clerk from the Hudson's Bay Company and a French trader. They are both trying to persuade the Aboriginal people to trade with their companies.

Which company would you choose? Why?

The North West Company

The coat of arms of the North West Company used many symbols of the fur trade.

While the English traded at their posts on Hudson Bay, the French continued to trade furs along the St. Lawrence River and west of the Great Lakes.

In the 1750s, The Seven Years' War broke out between France and England. When the war ended, England had won control of the French settlements. Some Scottish fur traders in New York decided to move to Montréal to run the fur trade there. The St. Lawrence River was the best route to the fur country, and they believed they could make more money.

The Scots and French made good partners. The Scots had money to pay for fur-trading trips. They knew people in Europe who wanted to buy furs.

The Scots used the French trading posts and took over the French fur-trading companies. The Scots hired many expert French traders called **voyageurs** to trade with the Aboriginal Peoples. Some of the voyageurs had learned to speak Aboriginal languages and married Aboriginal women. The voyageurs transported the furs back to the merchants. They knew the routes inland to the best fur country. Some voyageurs travelled thousands of kilometres by canoe to explore and trade in areas of Canada where no Europeans had ever been before. The French had learned the value of canoes from the Aboriginal Peoples.

By the 1780s, there were many small fur-trading companies in Montréal. They competed with one another. Some of the merchants decided to join together to improve their business. In 1783, they formed the North West Company. Many Nor'Westers, as the traders came to be called, spent the winter collecting furs from the Aboriginal Peoples.

The Montréal merchants had problems getting supplies and goods to their trading posts in the West. Canoe travel was expensive and took a long time. To solve this problem, the Nor'Westers built a large trading centre on Lake Superior called Fort William. Each summer, merchants from Montréal took supplies and trading goods to Fort William. There they met their **wintering partners**, who came with canoes filled with furs from the inland posts.

The North West Company and the Hudson's Bay Company became bitter **rivals**. The North West Company was soon getting twice as many furs as the Hudson's Bay Company. After a hundred years of the Aboriginal Peoples coming to its trading posts on the bay, the Hudson's Bay Company had to change. It began to build inland trading posts, too.

Finding Information

1. What symbols on the coat of arms are still used to describe Canada today?

2. Use a dictionary to look up the word located at the top of the North West Company's coat of arms—perseverance. How does this word relate to the North West Company's rivalry with the Hudson's Bay Company?

The Life of a Voyageur

Voyageurs who paddled canoes loaded with trade goods and furs lived a life of adventure and hard work. They often travelled across the country in groups called fur brigades. Here is how one voyageur might have described his life in his journal. What problems did he have?

June 7, 1792

We are five days' journey away from Fort William. It has been a long, tiring trip for all ten of us, but especially for me. I am thirty-seven, too old for this life. Where are all my friends who became voyageurs with me long ago? They have quit or become worn out. Some have died by drowning or from working too hard.

We travelled a long way today, so we stopped before sundown. We camped in a clearing by the river where there are few mosquitoes. We had been paddling for almost fifteen hours. We stopped for ten-minute breaks every hour. That was all that kept me going.

My arms are always sore from paddling. The weight of the pack that I carry on portages makes my back sore too. Today, as we walked on wet rocks near the rapids, I slipped and fell in the water. Thank goodness it was shallow. If it had been deep, the weight of the pack would have taken me under before my friends could save me.

It is starting to rain again, but the campfire is burning well. I am lying under my overturned canoe, listening to the noise the river makes and my friends laughing and singing.

Why do I love this work? It pays twice what a skilled worker earns in Montréal. I have seen much of this country and met many people. In spite of the hardships, I have had good times with my partners.

This painting by Frances Ann Hopkins is called "Voyageurs at Dawn." The men used overturned canoes as a temporary shelter.

Changes Caused by the Fur Trade

The Europeans traded for furs they could sell in Europe. The Aboriginal Peoples wanted items they could use everyday, such as pots and knives.

What do you think?

Which goods can you see that the Aboriginal Peoples might have wanted?

The Aboriginal Peoples of eastern Canada were the first to meet explorers and traders from Europe. The explorers returned to Europe with stories about the new people and lands they had seen. They brought back new food that Europeans had never eaten before. Corn, beans, squash, and tobacco were plants from North America. The Aboriginal Peoples acted as guides for the explorers. They taught the Europeans what they knew about the land. They showed them how to use canoes, moccasins, snowshoes, and toboggans.

Traders came to get furs from the new lands. They built trading posts where Aboriginal Peoples could bring their furs. When the fur trade began, it fit well into Aboriginal ways of life. The Aboriginal Peoples had always hunted and traded for what they needed. The fur trade brought them metal tools and weapons that replaced those of stone and bone. Iron cooking pots and copper kettles replaced those made of clay, skin, bark, or wood. Guns replaced bows and arrows. Hunting for food became quicker and easier.

As the fur trade grew, Aboriginal ways of life began to change. For some groups, such as the Mi'kmaq, hunting and trapping for furs to trade replaced summer food gathering and other activities. Aboriginal groups that changed in this way became dependent on trade goods such as clothing from Europe. The European clothing was not as warm or well-suited to Canada's climate as the clothing the Aboriginal Peoples had made themselves from furs and hides.

The diseases brought from Europe were new to the Aboriginal Peoples. Many Aboriginal people became ill and died from European diseases such as measles.

The fur trade caused changes in Aboriginal Peoples' beliefs. New beliefs changed the special bond the Aboriginal Peoples had with the animals they hunted.

The fur trade also changed some Aboriginal ways of keeping order. Instead of picking their leaders because of their wisdom, some chiefs were chosen because of their skill as fur traders.

Competition between the rival fur-trading companies caused conflict between the Huron and the Iroquois. The English made a partnership with the Iroquois, and the French made a partnership with the Huron. As the English and French fought, so did their Aboriginal partners.

In Summary

1. The first Europeans who came to Canada began to trade with the Aboriginal Peoples. At first, the Europeans wanted fresh food in exchange for their metal tools and other goods. Soon they learned that the Aboriginal Peoples had furs to trade. Merchants in Europe wanted to buy furs.

2. Some Europeans became full-time fur traders. The traders developed fur-trading partnerships with Aboriginal Peoples. Many of the traders explored and made maps of Canada with the help of their Aboriginal guides.

3. The Europeans started fur-trading companies. The English began the Hudson's Bay Company, which traded in the area around Hudson Bay. The French had many smaller companies. The voyageurs travelled inland to trade, and took furs back to the settlements in the St. Lawrence valley. Later on, the Scots and the French also started a large company, the North West Company.

4. The fur trade caused many changes in the way Europeans and Aboriginal Peoples lived.

Reliving the Past

1. Choose several members of your class to act as explorers or fur traders. Have each person explain to the class why his or her work was important to the fur trade. Have members of the class vote to decide which person was most important to the fur trade.

2. The Hudson's Bay Company traders had to write reports to the company officials in England. Pretend you are a trader and write a short report describing how you traded with a group of Cree people.

Beaver was the kind of fur the Europeans wanted most. They also traded for the furs of seals, foxes, moose, and other fur-bearing animals.

Part Four

Missionaries

When explorers and traders returned to Europe with stories of the people they met in the new land, some Europeans felt they had a special duty to teach their Christian beliefs to the Aboriginal Peoples. These Europeans were called missionaries.

The missionaries belonged to different **religious orders** in Europe. Several orders sent missionaries to Canada. One order was the Récollets. Another was the Jesuits. More Jesuits came to Canada than members of any other order.

The early missionaries who came to Canada were from France. They built mission settlements among the Aboriginal Peoples of eastern Canada. The missions were built in Acadia, along the St. Lawrence River, and among the Huron people near the Great Lakes.

The missionaries wrote reports about the Aboriginal Peoples they met. These reports described the Aboriginal Peoples' ways of life, beliefs, and the way they kept order in their groups. Many of the missionaries learned several Aboriginal languages. The records left by the missionaries help us learn about Aboriginal Peoples in early Canada.

The missionaries travelled to the homes of the Aboriginal Peoples. There they built mission settlements.

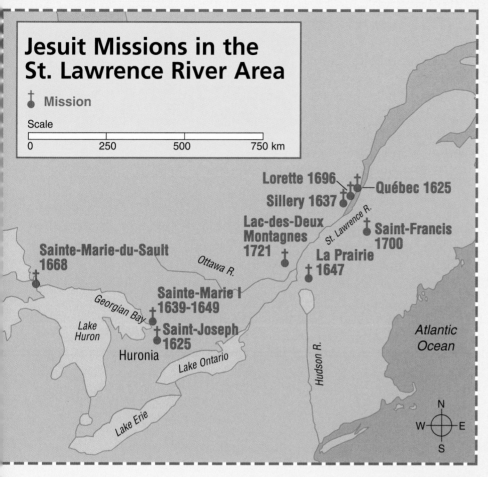

Jesuit Missions in the St. Lawrence River Area

✝ Mission

Scale
0   250   500   750 km

Lorette 1696
Sillery 1637
Québec 1625
Lac-des-Deux Montagnes 1721
St. Lawrence R.
Saint-Francis 1700
La Prairie 1647
Sainte-Marie-du-Sault 1668
Ottawa R.
Georgian Bay
Sainte-Marie I 1639-1649
Saint-Joseph 1625
Lake Huron
Huronia
Lake Ontario
Hudson R.
Atlantic Ocean
Lake Erie

N
W⊕E
S

During the 1600s and 1700s, the missionaries lived and worked with the Aboriginal Peoples and the settlers. They built missions in the areas where the Aboriginal Peoples lived. This map shows when some of the larger missions were built by the Jesuits before 1750.

The area of Huronia had a number of smaller missions that are not shown. Saint-Joseph was one of the first and the largest in the area. Sainte-Marie was burned to the ground in 1649.

Learning from Maps

Using the map on this page, make a time line showing the construction of Jesuit missions in the St. Lawrence River area.

Notre-Dame-des-Victories is a church located in Québec City. It was built in 1690 and is still standing today.

Missionaries in Acadia

The first French missionary who came to Canada was a **Roman Catholic** named Abbé Jessé Fléché. In 1610, he came to the French settlement at Port-Royal with the early fur traders. He stayed at Port-Royal for a year. While he was there, he **baptized** a Mi'kmaq chief named Membertou and twenty members of the chief's family. Fléché returned to France in 1611.

Two Jesuit **priests** arrived in Port-Royal in 1611. They soon found that they needed to learn the Mi'kmaq language. One of the priests, Father Pierre Biard, stayed at Port-Royal. He learned the Mi'kmaq language from a young boy. Father Enemond Massé lived with a group of Mi'kmaq people so he could learn their language. The missionaries taught the Mi'kmaq people Christian prayers and beliefs. They baptized some of the adults and children. After the Jesuits had won the trust of the Mi'kmaq, they decided to leave Acadia to start another Jesuit mission.

The missionaries and the settlers at Port-Royal interacted frequently with the Mi'kmaq. The missionaries wanted to replace the Aboriginal Peoples' spiritual beliefs with their own Christian values.

What do you think?

1. Which objects might the missionaries have given to the Mi'kmaq?

2. What objects might the Mi'kmaq have traded their furs to receive?

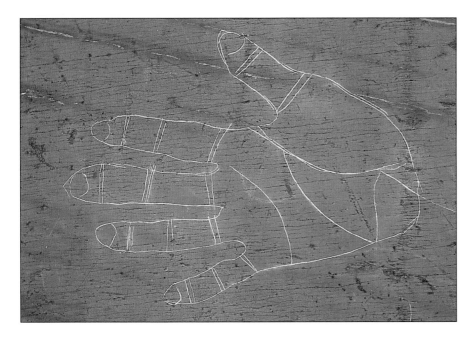

These petroglyphs, or stone carvings, can be seen at Kejimkujik National Park in Nova Scotia. The park has been made a National Historic site because of its many cultural features.

Hands are represented in artwork throughout the world and throughout time, probably because they are an easy way for the artist to leave a personal identification. This hand has been drawn in detail with palm and fingerprint lines.

In 1676, a Récollet missionary named Father Chrétien Le Clercq came to the Gaspé area. He wrote in a report that the Mi'kmaq language was "very beautiful and very rich." He was the first European to notice that the Mi'kmaq had a kind of writing.

The Mi'kmaq people used small drawings called pictographs to show things and ideas. Le Clercq saw that the Mi'kmaq children made marks on birchbark with charcoal while he taught them about Christianity. These marks helped them remember what he had taught them. Le Clercq helped the Mi'kmaq invent more pictographs so they could write down the Christian ideas he discussed.

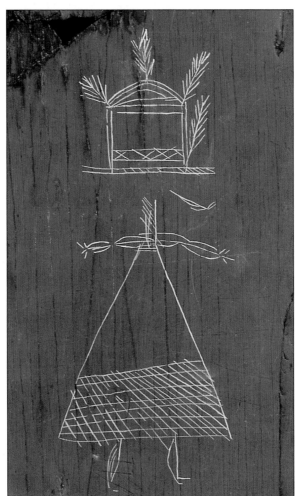

The long coat and square hat have been part of traditional Mi'kmaq dress from the mid-eighteenth century to the present. The clothing style has its origin in European styles of clothing.

What Should Father Le Jeune Do?

In 1632, Father Paul Le Jeune arrived at Québec with a group of Jesuit missionaries. He was the leader of the Jesuits in Canada from 1632 to 1639. He went with the Montagnais on their winter hunt his first year at Québec. He knew he would not be able to teach the Montagnais about Christianity until he could speak their language. Le Jeune learned the Montagnais language, but he was not able to change their beliefs. When he returned to Québec, he tried to think of the best way to teach Christian beliefs to the different groups of Aboriginal Peoples who lived near the St. Lawrence River. He also thought about other ways the Jesuits might be able to help the Aboriginal Peoples. Before he decided what to do, he considered several plans.

PLANS	REASONS	QUESTIONS
To teach the Aboriginal children how to become Christians	Many of the older people will not give up their old beliefs. Maybe the children should go to school away from their parents. Then they might listen to the missionaries.	Who will we find to teach the young children?
To settle the Aboriginal hunters who move about from place to place	If the Aboriginal Peoples farmed, they would stay in one place. Then they might have more time to listen to our ideas.	How can we persuade the Aboriginal hunters to settle down and learn to farm?
To care for the sick, the poor, the old, and the orphans	The Aboriginal Peoples and the settlers need a hospital. There is nobody to look after the sick and the poor. Giving help will cost a lot of money. Most of the settlers are too poor to help.	Where can we find enough money to pay for these much needed services?

If you were Father Le Jeune, which plan or plans would you choose? Give reasons for your choice.

Father Le Jeune's Plans

While Father Le Jeune was the leader of the Jesuits, he decided to carry out all three plans.

Le Jeune's first plan was to teach the Aboriginal children in the area how to become Christians. Soon after he arrived in Québec, he began to teach. His first pupils were a child in a French family and an Aboriginal boy. In 1635, the Jesuits started a school for boys in Québec. In 1636, there were twenty students in the school. The Ursuline nuns also started a school in Québec. It was the first school for girls. Both the schools were for Aboriginal and settlers' children.

In 1637, Le Jeune tried to make his second plan work. He began to gather the Aboriginal hunters so he could teach them to be farmers. A rich Frenchman named Noel de Sillery read about Le Jeune's plan. He gave Le Jeune some land near Québec. This land was set aside for Aboriginal Peoples who became Christians. It was the first Aboriginal **reserve** in Canada. The plan was not very successful. Only a few Aboriginal families came to live in the houses Le Jeune built at Sillery.

Le Jeune's plan to care for the sick was more successful. In 1639, some French Ursuline nuns arrived in Québec. They helped start the first hospital in Québec.

To raise money for the missionaries and to let other people in the Jesuit order learn about what he was doing, Le Jeune wrote reports about the people and events in Canada. He asked other missionaries to write about their life and travels in Canada. These reports, called the *Jesuit Relations*, were sent to France each year. In them, Le Jeune and the other French missionaries described how they lived. They also wrote about the Aboriginal Peoples they met in Canada.

Many French people read the *Jesuit Relations*. Sometimes, the missionaries wrote about problems they were having and of things they needed to have sent to them. The *Jesuit Relations* inspired many French people to give money and land for the missions. Much of what we know about the Aboriginal Peoples and the Europeans who lived in early Canada comes from the *Jesuit Relations*.

Father Le Jeune stopped being the leader of the Jesuits in Canada in 1639. He stayed in Canada for another ten years before he returned to France in 1649. During his last decade in Canada, he worked as a missionary at many communities along the St. Lawrence River.

Father Paul Le Jeune was leader of the Jesuits in Canada in the 1630s.

Finding Information

Name two important contributions the *Jesuit Relations* made to early Canada.

Father Jean de Brébeuf

Father Jean de Brébeuf was the founder of the Jesuit mission in Huronia. In June 1625, he arrived at Québec with a group of Jesuit priests and their helpers. Brébeuf spent five months travelling with a group of Montagnais people his first winter.

In 1626, Brébeuf was told to go to the lands where the Huron lived. In July 1626, he set off for Huronia. The trip was almost 1 300 kilometres from Québec. Brébeuf travelled by canoe. It was a long, hard trip, with many portages. The Jesuits were also bothered by mosquitoes. It took almost a month to get to Huronia.

Brébeuf lived with the Huron for the next three years. He studied their language and way of life. His reports show his love and respect for the Huron people.

In 1629, the English were trying to win control of Canada. After they captured Québec, all the Jesuit missionaries were sent back to France.

In 1633, Brébeuf returned to Canada. Father Paul Le Jeune sent him to build a new, lasting mission among the Huron people. He arrived in 1634 and built a mission called Saint-Joseph I. Later he built two other settlements, including Saint-Joseph II.

During the years that Brébeuf lived in Huronia, he wrote a dictionary of the Huron words he learned. He **translated** Christian prayers into the Huron language.

During the 1630s, many of the Huron died of diseases such as **smallpox** and measles, brought by the newcomers from Europe. The Jesuits believed that if people died before they were baptized, their souls would be lost forever. To save souls, they baptized many sick people just before they died. The Huron saw that many of their people died soon after they were baptized. They blamed the missionaries for the deaths of their people. They began to threaten the priests, who had to leave Huronia for a time.

In 1644, Brébeuf returned to the Huron just as they were facing another threat. The Iroquois, supplied with guns from their English partners, were attacking the Huron to gain control of the fur-trading route to the West. The Iroquois were unable to travel through the Huron country to trade with other Aboriginal Peoples farther west. The Huron did not have any guns. The French refused to give their partners guns until they became Catholic. When the Iroquois attacked in 1649, almost all of the Huron people were killed. Brébeuf and several other Jesuits were also killed.

The Huron Carol

First stanza in Huron

Esteiaron de tsonoue,
Jesous ahatonhia.
Onna-ouate oua d'oki
n'ou ouanda skoua en tak.
En nonchien skouatchi
hotak, n'on ouandi
lonra chata,
Jesous ahatonhia, Jesous
ahatonhia, Jesous
ahatonhia.

First stanza in English

'Twas in the moon of winter time when all the birds had fled, That mighty Gitchi Manitou sent angel choirs instead; Before their light the stars grew dim and wand'ring hunters heard the hymn: "Jesus your king is born, Jesus is born: in excelsis gloria!"

Using the tune of an old French Christmas carol, Brébeuf told the Christmas story in the Huron language.

The Destruction of Huronia

During the 1630s, the Jesuits built several mission settlements in Huronia. In 1639, they built a large mission settlement called Sainte-Marie-aux-Hurons. It had a **chapel,** homes, carpentry and iron-working shops, and a hospital. Outside the palisade was a farm.

During the 1640s, the Iroquois attacked Huronia because of the conflict caused by the fur trade. Jesuit reports describe these difficult years. This account of the final destruction of Huronia is taken from different Jesuit journals.

1648

We have heard the news of Father Antoine Daniel's glorious death in July of this year at the hands of the Iroquois. Just after the usual prayers at sunrise, the people of Saint-Joseph's mission heard the enemy's war cry. Terror and sorrow were soon everywhere. Many rushed to be baptized in the face of death. Father Daniel was forced to dip his handkerchief in the holy water and to sprinkle the whole group clustered around him in the little church. Like a good shepherd, he blocked the way and held off the enemy to let some of his flock escape. At last he fell, killed by a **musket** shot and pierced by arrows. The Iroquois then set the church on fire. Some of the Huron reached places of safety. Others were taken captive by the Iroquois.

1649

The Iroquois raiders keep burning villages to the ground. Over 3 000 Huron have left their villages for the shelter, food, and hospital care they can get at Sainte-Marie-aux-Hurons. We have provided a safe harbour for the Huron. Hundreds have turned to God in this disastrous time. The deaths of Fathers Jean de Brébeuf and Gabriel Lalemant in March of this year have sent two more holy **martyrs** to God.

The smoke rising into the spring sky from the burning Huron villages can be seen here at Sainte-Marie. More terror fills the hearts of the Huron as survivors from the ruined villages trickle in through our gates.

1650

We had to leave our homes in Sainte-Marie to escape the Iroquois. We set the mission on fire to prevent the Iroquois from using it. We were all filled with sorrow as we watched our beautiful village being destroyed. Then we embarked with three hundred Christian Huron families to a refuge on Saint-Joseph's Island. Our winter has been difficult, for food is scarce and disease has struck the people hard.

Which words make the writers' point of view clear?
Why are there no written records from the point of view of the Huron or the Iroquois? How did the Huron and Iroquois remember historical information?
What reasons might there have been for the fighting between the Iroquois on one side and the Jesuits and Hurons on the other?

Marie de l'Incarnation

Sister Marie de l'Incarnation decided to come to Canada from her home in France after reading the *Jesuit Relations*.

What do you think?

Why do you think it was important that early missionaries wrote about their experiences in Canada?

While the Jesuits worked in Huronia, other religious people came to live in the St. Lawrence River valley. Many came in answer to Le Jeune's request for help. Some of them were women.

Sister Marie de l'Incarnation was the first leader of the Ursuline nuns in Canada. Before Sister Marie became a nun, her name had been Marie Guyart. She was the daughter of a baker in France. She had wanted to become a nun when she was a child, but her parents wanted her to marry. When she grew up, she was married and had a son, but her husband died after only two years of marriage. She entered a **convent**, and her son went to live with her sister. In 1633 she chose a religious name, Marie de l'Incarnation.

In May 1639, Sister Marie and her group of Ursuline nuns sailed to Canada. They came to the settlement at Québec to teach young French and Aboriginal girls. Their first home and school was a rough, two-room shelter. Wind and rain blew through cracks in the walls and the roof, making it hard to keep candles lit.

The little school taught general knowledge, sewing, music, and manners. When it got crowded, the nuns moved to a new building. The new school also had drawbacks. Sister Marie wrote to her son in France, "The beds are in wood closets and close like cupboards, and although they are lined with cloth, one can hardly get warm."

Sister Marie was a calm, determined person. She took disaster in stride. The first winter she was there, smallpox swept through the settlement. Another year, the convent burned down in the middle of winter, and Sister Marie had to find a new home for herself, the nuns, and her students. When the settlement was rocked by an earthquake, Sister Marie tried to look on the bright side. She wrote, "At the same time that God shook the rocks and the mountains of this wild country, he shook the souls of men."

Sister Marie looked after the business of the convent and taught her students. She also learned several Aboriginal languages. She wrote what she had learned into dictionaries. Sister Marie wrote many letters to people in France. Her letters were filled with information about the events, habits, and customs of the people who lived in the St. Lawrence River valley.

Sister Marie de l'Incarnation died when she was seventy-three. The convent she founded over three hundred years ago still stands in Québec City today. In 1980, she was named Blessed Marie de l'Incarnation by the Roman Catholic church.

The Mission at Ville-Marie

The Jesuit reports sent from Canada aroused great interest among wealthy people in France. Some of them formed a Roman Catholic missionary society in 1640. The society intended to teach Christian beliefs to the Aboriginal Peoples in Canada. The society also wanted to provide schools and hospitals for the Aboriginal Peoples. Paul de Chomedey, **Sieur** de Maisonneuve, was chosen to build a new mission settlement up the river from Québec.

Maisonneuve set sail from France in 1641. With him sailed a group of fifty people who wanted to help start the new mission on the island of Montréal. One of the members of Maisonneuve's group was Jeanne Mance, a nurse who hoped to build a hospital for the Aboriginal Peoples.

When the settlers reached Québec, the people there advised them not to go any farther. The spot where they planned to build the new settlement lay on the Iroquois trading route. It would be in danger of attack by the Iroquois. After spending the winter in Québec, Maisonneuve insisted that they go on. In spring of 1642, they reached the mission site.

Soon after they arrived, the missionaries began to build a fort. They built a high wall and placed a cannon at each corner. They dug a deep ditch, or moat, around the wall. Inside, they built houses and a chapel. They planted peas and corn. They began to meet the Algonquin people who lived nearby. In August, twelve more settlers came to live at the mission. On August 15th, the new community held a celebration and named their settlement Ville-Marie.

As the settlers in Québec had warned, Ville-Marie was soon attacked by the Iroquois people. Ville-Marie blocked an important Iroquois trading route to the Ottawa River. Jeanne Mance gave Maisonneuve money meant for her hospital to hire soldiers to defend the mission.

For several years, the Iroquois tried to make the settlers move away from Ville-Marie. Sometimes the settlers thought they might have to move, but people in France sent soldiers to help defend the mission. The Iroquois were unable to protect their trading route. The settlement at Ville-Marie began to grow.

Mance raised money in France for a hospital at Ville-Marie. Soon after she arrived, she built a four-room hospital outside the fort. She spent thirty years nursing sick and wounded French and Aboriginal people.

Marguerite Bourgeoys

In spite of the conflict between the French and the Iroquois, missionaries continued to come to Canada from France.

In 1652, Marguerite Bourgeoys met Maisonneuve while he was visiting France. Bourgeoys was a nun in a French convent. Maisonneuve visited the convent to see his sister, who was also a nun there. Bourgeoys asked Maisonneuve if she could come to Ville-Marie. She wanted to start a school and a religious community there. Maisonneuve agreed to let her come.

Bourgeoys landed at Québec in 1653. When she arrived at Ville-Marie, she found there were no school-aged children. She worked hard for the next five years, ironing and washing for the sick and the poor. She also shared her food. Finally, she was able to open a school in a **stable**. There she taught reading, writing, and crafts.

As the school grew, more help was needed. Bourgeoys founded a religious community of teaching sisters. Her teachers did not wait inside the school for students to come to them. Instead, they travelled by canoe or on horseback to teach Aboriginal and French children in their homes along the St. Lawrence River.

In 1676, Bourgeoys opened a boarding school for girls in Ville-Marie and a school to teach home-making skills. She also began a mission school in the Aboriginal village of La Montagne.

Young women who came from France to marry settlers stayed at the school in Ville-Marie. Men from the French settlements came to meet the Frenchwomen and choose their wives. At the school, the women learned the skills they would need to keep house in the settlements after they got married.

During the time that Bourgeoys lived in Ville-Marie, it grew into an important centre. Fur traders and other settlers came to live there with the religious settlers. The village became known as Montréal instead of Ville-Marie.

Bourgeoys spent her last years in Montréal. Before her death in January 1700, the people of Montréal had come to believe she was a **saint**. In 1982, the Roman Catholic church recognized her achievements and named her a saint.

Bourgeoys was one of the early settlers at Ville-Marie. She became the first female Catholic saint who spent most of her life in Canada.

Kateri Tekakwitha, "Lily of the Mohawks"

Tekakwitha was born in a Mohawk village in 1656. When she was baptized as a Christian, she chose the name Kateri. People have reported many miracles taking place at her shrine in Caughnawaga. In 1980, the Roman Catholic church named her "among the blessed in heaven." Someday she may become the first Aboriginal woman to be named a saint.

This is how she might have described her life. What qualities might make people believe she was a saint?

My mother was Algonquin. She was brought up as a Christian by French settlers near Trois-Rivières. As part of the fur trade conflict, she was captured in an Iroquois attack in 1653 and taken to live at a Mohawk village. She married a Mohawk man there.

My parents died during a smallpox **epidemic** in 1660. I caught smallpox too, and barely survived. The disease scarred my face and made my eyes weak. My uncle, the chief of our village, adopted me.

In 1666, a French raiding party burned down our village. Our leader decided to make peace. During the peace talks, he asked for some missionaries to come to our lands. The next year, three Jesuits and two of their helpers came to our new village. I took care of them while they were there and listened carefully to their teachings. They told me about the work of the Ursuline nuns at Québec.

I wanted to become a Christian, but my uncle would not allow it. He wanted me to get married. I refused. For eight years, I endured his anger and tried to live a Christian life. When I was nineteen, a visiting priest baptized me. I took the name Kateri, meaning Catherine.

After I was baptized, my family and friends turned against me. They even said they would kill me unless I gave up my new beliefs.

I spent long hours in prayer at a little altar I built myself. Finally, in the fall of 1677, I managed to escape with some other Aboriginal Christians. We went to the Saint-Francois-Xavier mission near Montréal. There I met my mother's Christian teacher. He helped me as he helped my mother before me.

Kateri Tekakwitha always had poor health. She was only twenty-four when she died.

At first, I liked to spend time with my own people. I would go on winter hunting trips with them. Later on, I began to stay close to the mission all the time, with the Europeans. I didn't want to leave the church.

I wanted to become a nun. I dreamed of forming a community of Aboriginal nuns, but the Jesuits didn't like this idea.

I found great happiness helping others, but my health began to fail in 1680. I was not strong enough to carry out my dreams. I hope people will remember me after I die.

Peter Jones

Jones prepared the first translation of the Bible into Ojibwa.

It was many years before the Aboriginal Peoples became teachers of Christianity themselves. By that time, people had begun to settle farther west. Some of these people were English-speaking and members of **Protestant** churches. One of the earliest Aboriginal missionaries was Peter Jones.

Peter Jones was born in 1802 in a wigwam in what is now Ontario. His father was an American. His mother was the daughter of an Ojibwa chief. Their baby was named Kahkewaquonaby, which means "sacred feathers." His mother and her family taught him and his brother the skills of her people. The boys learned to hunt, fish, and paddle a canoe.

When Jones was fourteen, his father sent him to school to learn to read, write, and speak English. At school people called him Peter Jones. In the summers, he learned to farm. He thought he might like to become a fur trader when he grew up.

When he was twenty-one, something happened that changed his life. He went to a **Methodist** church meeting. There he decided to become a Christian and spend his life teaching others.

Jones began by teaching the people in his mother's village. The church and school he built became the centre of village life. The people liked him so much that they chose him to be chief. His brother and sister-in-law worked with him. They taught the people how to farm.

Jones often went on tours to raise money for his church. Those who heard him speak often wanted to help him. One group gave him a stove to heat his schoolhouse. Another group sent him a plough. When he travelled to England, people there came in large numbers to see his Aboriginal clothes and to hear him speak. He met King William IV and told him about life in Canada.

Whenever Aboriginal Christians in the area had problems, they came to Jones. When other settlers tried to take their land away, he spoke up for his people. He helped them to get tools and animals for their farms. He wrote letters and books on the needs of his people.

Jones continued to work and travel even when he felt sick. One rainy night, he rode more than thirty kilometres to a meeting. This made him ill and led to his death. The people he had helped held a huge funeral for him.

What do you think?

Why do you think Jones was a successful missionary?

In Summary

1. Missionaries from Europe came to the new land to teach the Christian religion to the Aboriginal Peoples.

2. The first missionaries went to Acadia. There they taught the Mi'kmaq people about Christian beliefs. Missionaries also went inland. They built missions along the St. Lawrence River and in Huronia. Brébeuf and other Jesuits lived with the Huron at the missions.

3. Missionaries learned many things about the Aboriginal Peoples. They learned that the Aboriginal Peoples had their own spiritual beliefs. They learned that the Mi'kmaq people had a kind of writing. Some missionaries learned Aboriginal languages and wrote dictionaries. Some of them translated Christian prayers and stories into Aboriginal languages. The missionaries wrote reports about the things they had learned.

4. Some Aboriginal Peoples preferred to keep their own spiritual beliefs. Others accepted Christianity. Some Aboriginal people became missionaries themselves and worked among their own people.

The Jesuits used Mi'kmaq pictographs to teach Christian prayers.

Reliving the Past

1. Hold a class discussion on the following question: How did the missionaries change the Aboriginal Peoples' way of life?

2. Role play a meeting between a Huron and a Jesuit. What might the Jesuit say to convince the Huron to become a Christian? What might the Huron say in reply?

Part Five

Settlers

For many years, England and France took fish, furs, and other resources from the lands they had claimed. Then, they decided to build settlements to keep control of these areas. They began to build **permanent** settlements in three main areas.

The English built fishing settlements in Newfoundland. The fishing settlements grew slowly. The English also built trading posts around Hudson Bay. However, settlers did not want to live at the trading posts because the climate was too harsh. These posts were built mainly for business.

The French built settlements on Canada's east coast. They called this area Acadia. They also built settlements along the St. Lawrence River and around the Great Lakes. This large area was known as **New France**.

As the years progressed, the French and English competed with each other to control the settlements. In the end, England won control over all the European settlements in Canada.

Most of the settlers were farmers. They obtained food by growing crops. Many settlers also worked in the fishing industry and in the fur trade. Some made a living in the **lumber** industry. The kind of settlements that grew in early Canada were linked to the land, climate, and resources in each area.

Part 5, "Settlers," shows how some of the first Europeans who moved to Canada lived. It tells about how they got along with other settlers and with the Aboriginal Peoples who lived near them.

In this painting by C.W. Jefferys, settlers are clearing land for a farm. Only some parts of Canada were well-suited for farming.

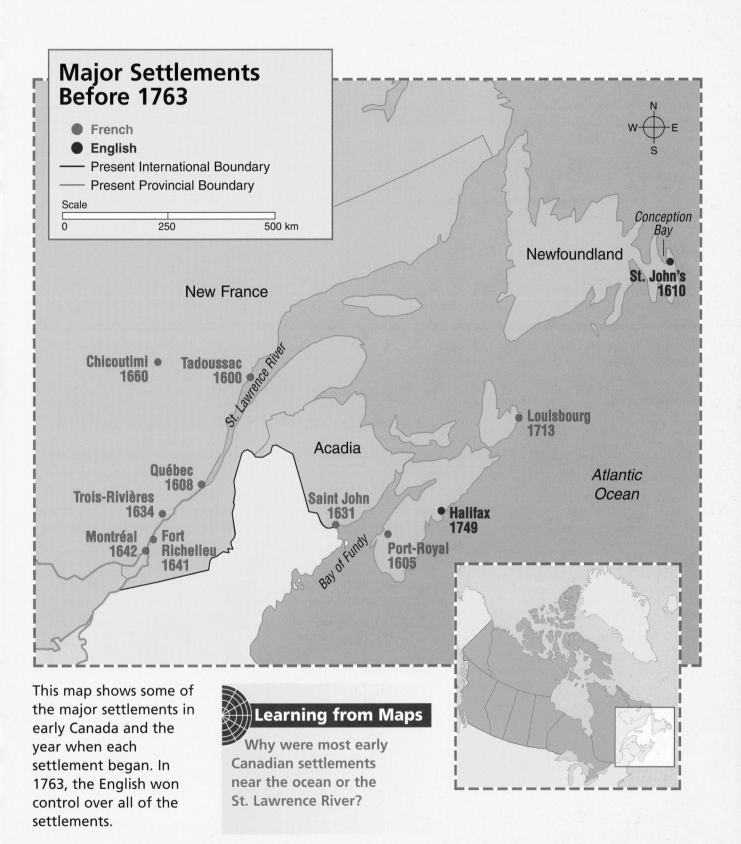

Major Settlements Before 1763

● French
● **English**
— Present International Boundary
— Present Provincial Boundary

Scale
0   250   500 km

New France

Conception Bay

Newfoundland

**St. John's
1610**

Chicoutimi ● **Tadoussac**
1660   **1600** ●

St. Lawrence River

Louisbourg
1713

Acadia

Atlantic Ocean

**Québec
1608** ●

**Trois-Rivières
1634** ●

**Saint John
1631** ●

● **Halifax
1749**

**Montréal
1642** ●   **Fort
Richelieu
1641**

Bay of Fundy

**Port-Royal
1605** ●

This map shows some of the major settlements in early Canada and the year when each settlement began. In 1763, the English won control over all of the settlements.

Learning from Maps

Why were most early Canadian settlements near the ocean or the St. Lawrence River?

Fishing Settlements in Newfoundland

The French and English preserved fish in different ways. The French anchored their ships offshore. The crews fished for months. They salted the cod heavily and stored it on the ships. The crews rarely went ashore, except to get fresh water and firewood.

The English did not have as much salt as the French. They cleaned and lightly salted the cod. Then they dried it in the sun on racks on the shore. The dried cod was packed in barrels. It did not spoil easily, so it could be shipped for sale to warmer countries. This drawing shows a fishing station on the shore.

What do you think?

1. **Which fishing method used by the Europeans was more likely to bring them into contact with the Aboriginal Peoples? Why?**

2. **Why did English merchants not have any lasting settlements in Newfoundland?**

During the 1500s, many fishers from European countries sailed to the Grand Banks each summer to fish. Some English captains began to leave a few crew members on shore each winter to look after their fishing equipment and drying racks. Some people spent winter after winter in Newfoundland. They built houses and Newfoundland became their home.

In 1610, John Guy came to Newfoundland to start a settlement. Thirty-nine people came with him. They intended to run the **fishery**. They built one of the first English settlements in Canada at Cuper's Cove on Conception Bay. The settlement grew quickly. After a year, there were sixty settlers. During the spring and summer, settlers salted and dried fish. They also planted vegetables, although Newfoundland was not suited for large farms. The fishers who did not live there scornfully called them "planters."

The English merchants did not want settlers year-round in Newfoundland. They wanted to earn all the profits from the fishery themselves. To scare the settlers away, they sent gangs to tear down their houses. Some of the settlers hid in **coves**. They built new homes without chimneys so smoke could not give their location away. In spite of the merchants, communities slowly grew along the coast of Newfoundland.

People with Different Ideas

The Beothuk were the Aboriginal people who lived in Newfoundland when fishers and settlers first visited the area. In the beginning, they had little contact with the Europeans, but there was conflict as European settlements grew.

BEOTHUK HUNTER

I don't understand these newcomers. They arrive in ships every spring, but stay only a few months. They leave their equipment on the beach as if they don't want it. If I leave something on someone else's land, it means I no longer need it or I am presenting it as a gift. When I take what they have left, they shoot at me with their cannons or their smaller guns. They do the same if I take some of their fish, even though they have more than they need to eat. My people always share food with anyone who needs it.

Now some of these people are starting to build houses and stay all year. A few of them are on the northeast coast, my favourite summer hunting spot. That's where I hunt seals, gather birds' eggs, and catch fish. There won't be enough food for my family if I can't do these things. The caribou I kill inland in the winter won't last all year long.

ENGLISH SETTLER

I don't understand the Beothuk people. When we leave fishing equipment on the shore for the winter, it's gone when we return in the spring. They even take the fish from our drying racks.

I've decided to build a cabin, plant a garden, and live here all year round. But I'm afraid. The Beothuk don't look or dress the way we settlers do. I don't understand their behaviour. They mainly stay in the woods and don't live the way I do. I'm afraid they might hurt me and my family. I'll be sure to be prepared in case they come to take our things or attack us.

What do you think were the reasons for conflict between the Beothuk and Europeans? How could conflict have been avoided?

Farming Settlements in Acadia

The first farming settlements in Canada were built by French settlers on the Atlantic coast. The French area, called Acadia, included the areas now known as Nova Scotia, Prince Edward Island, and New Brunswick, and part of the Gaspé Peninsula.

Settlers began coming from France in the early 1600s. They wanted to trade furs with the Mi'kmaq and Maliseet peoples. None of the trading posts made enough money to survive, but each time a trading post failed, a few settlers stayed in Acadia to start farms. French settlers arrived until the late 1600s.

There was rich soil in many parts of Acadia. Fertile soil was contained in the **marshlands** that lay along the Bay of Fundy, Chignecto Bay, and the Minas Basin. The marshlands extended far inland along the rivers. There were plenty of forests on land and fish and shellfish in the ocean. Acadia was a land rich in resources.

The new settlers started farms. They cleared fields and grew crops. They also fished and hunted. They made some money in the fur trade and began a lumber industry.

This painting shows an evening's entertainment at Port-Royal, one of the earliest settlements in Acadia. The settlers formed the Order of Good Cheer to arrange feasts and plays to amuse themselves.

The Acadians provided most of their own food. They grew vegetables such as peas, potatoes, turnips, carrots, and beans. They caught fish in the rivers and the ocean. The Mi'kmaq people taught the first settlers how to hunt moose, deer, and bears. They also showed the Acadians how to trap smaller animals such as rabbits. They showed the settlers which wild plants and berries were safe to eat. In the marshlands, the Acadians grew hay and grain for dairy cattle. The Acadians used milk from the cattle to make cream, butter, and cheese.

Everyday clothing was made from **flax** and wool. Acadian settlers bought cloth from the English settlers who lived to the south. They also wove some cloth themselves. They wore flat shoes they made from sealskins and moose hides. When ships came from France, Acadians bought goods from French merchants.

Acadians often settled near the ocean because it was a means of transportation and a source of food. The nearby forests provided trees for houses and firewood.

The Acadians in this painting by Azor Vienneau are building a **dike**. Acadians invented a kind of dike that allowed overflowing sea water to drain off their farmland. The dikes kept many hectares of marshland dry enough for Acadian farmers to grow hay, wheat, oats, barley, and rye. They also raised cattle and grew fruits and vegetables.

Competing for Acadia

France and England competed with each other to control Acadia. Control of the area passed back and forth between France and England many times during the 1600s and 1700s. Often, wars in Europe decided who controlled Acadia.

In 1713, a peace treaty in Europe divided Acadia between the English and the French. The French kept present-day New Brunswick, Prince Edward Island, and Cape Breton Island, but the English took the area they had begun to call Nova Scotia.

The English immediately demanded an **oath** of loyalty from the Acadians in Nova Scotia. However, the Acadians did not want to swear this oath. They would only agree to be **neutral**. The English accepted this for a time, but they were afraid the Acadians would help the French if war broke out again. In 1755, the English forced all the Acadians to leave their homes in Nova Scotia. Some Acadians scattered along the east coast. In later years, some of the Acadians returned to live in Nova Scotia.

As English and Scottish settlers moved to Nova Scotia during the 1700s, they started new settlements along the coast. The settlers moved onto the land where the Mi'kmaq people lived. As forests were cleared for farms, the Mi'kmaq way of life changed. The settlers often built farms near the best fishing spots, where the Mi'kmaq had their summer camps. The Mi'kmaq had to find other ways to live. Some began to make and sell birchbark baskets. Others went to work for the settlers. Some Mi'kmaq worked in the fishing and lumber industries and others worked as guides.

After France lost Nova Scotia to England, the French decided to build a fortress on Cape Breton Island to guard the entrance to the Gulf of St. Lawrence and their other settlements. The fort at Louisbourg has been rebuilt to look as it did in the 1700s. It is now a museum.

People with Different Ideas

Many French settlers lived in Acadia when England and France fought for control over the area. Most of the Acadians stayed out of the fighting. Acadia, not France, was their home. However, the English did not trust the Acadians. In 1755, the English ordered the Acadians in Nova Scotia to leave their homes. Some went to France. Others moved to other French settlements. Some hid in the woods and returned when the fighting was over. Others went to the French territory in the United States.

AN ENGLISH ARMY OFFICER

When I attacked a French fort near Nova Scotia recently, my men found some Acadians fighting beside the French forces. If they fought there, they might fight for the French at their large forts along the St. Lawrence River. There are so many of them they could easily win.

I have asked the Acadians in Nova Scotia to swear an oath of loyalty to our king, George II, but they refuse. So I have ordered that they be forced to leave this settlement. They must go live in other places so they will no longer be a threat to our settlement. We have tried to keep Acadian families together, so as not to cause any hardship.

AN ACADIAN FARMER

The English have forced my family and me to leave our farm. My family has lived in Acadia for over a hundred years. We have done nothing to deserve such treatment. I never fought against the English. I just wanted to live in peace on my land.

I refuse to swear an oath of loyalty because, if I did, they might put me in the army. Then I might have to go fight against the French.

The English made me move to a place where most people speak English, not French. I was separated from my wife and children when I was loaded onto a boat. I can't find out what has become of them.

Until the day I die, I will never forget what the English did. I will always remember.

How do you think the Acadians felt when they were forced to leave their homes?
How might this make the Acadians feel about the English?

Settlers in New France

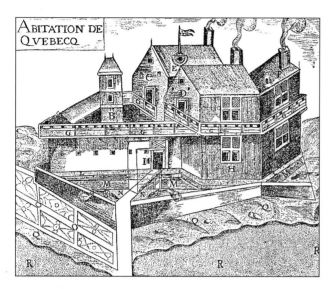

Champlain was considered an expert mapmaker and the founder of New France. This is one of his early drawings of Québec.

Acadia was not the only location for French settlements. The French also built communities along the St. Lawrence River valley in New France. The soil was rich and the river served as a road. Many French settlers started their farms on the lowlands bordering the river.

The king of France thought the resources of New France would be a source of wealth for France. The settlers would send **raw materials** to France and they would buy finished goods from French merchants. To help New France grow, the king sent soldiers to end the wars with the English and their trading partners, the Iroquois. He also sent more settlers to farm.

Towns began to grow in the river valley. The two largest towns were Québec and Montréal. Québec started as a fur-trading post but it soon grew to a town of importance. The governors of New France and the Roman Catholic bishop lived there. Québec was a port city. Furs were loaded onto ships and sent to France to be sold. Montréal became a fur-trading centre because other river routes joined the St. Lawrence River nearby. The fur traders and Aboriginal Peoples could easily bring their furs there.

The king of France gave pieces of land to important people if they promised to be loyal to him. They had to pay **taxes** and find farmers to clear and settle the land. The people who owned the land were called **seigneurs** and this way of owning land was called the seigneurial system.

Each seigneur divided his piece of land into small farms that

Thomas Davies' painting, "View from Chateau-Richer," shows a view of the St. Lawrence Lowlands. He painted it in about 1785. The **structures** in the river and on the marshes are eel traps.

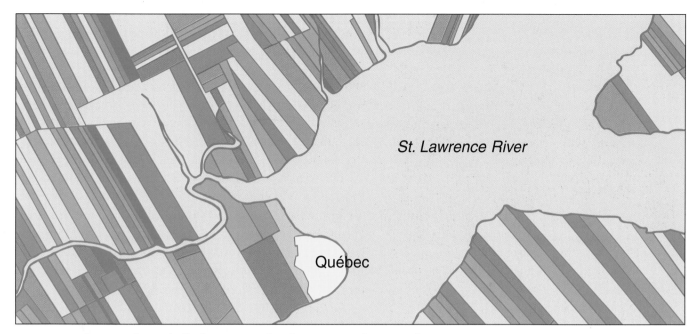

This drawing shows how the area around Québec was divided into many long, narrow farms.

were rented to settlers, or **habitants**. The farms were long and narrow. The land was divided so that each farm bordered the river. The farmers built their homes along the river, which was used as a transportation route. Since the houses were close together, the settlers felt they were part of a community.

The habitants of New France grew most of their own food. They made most of their clothes and furniture. They built their own houses. They baked bread in outdoor clay ovens.

Farmers grew wheat, barley, and oats. They paid a fee to grind these grains into flour at the seigneur's mill. Families sold extra grain in Montréal or Québec. There they bought goods they could not produce. Most families bought molasses, cloth, spices, pots, and pans. Much of the habitants' clothing was made by the women. Most cloth was handwoven. Scraps of cloth and old clothing were made into quilts and rugs.

Farmers in New France usually built their homes from trees cut on their farms. Some families built thick-walled houses with stones they had picked out of their fields. The steep roofs were covered with wooden shingles. A window was built into the roof to give some light to the attic bedroom where the children often slept.

The king of France allowed only Roman Catholics to settle in New France. Each family paid a tax, called a tithe, to the church. The tithe was usually one-tenth of a family's income. It was often paid in grain or food.

Farm life in New France was peaceful. The people lived in small communities. Everyone knew everyone else, and many families were related by marriage. The priest or seigneur tried to settle disputes by talking to the people involved. In larger settlements, the seigneur set up a court. If a problem could not be solved to everyone's satisfaction, an appeal was made to the higher court in the town of Québec.

What do you think?

Why was it important for farmers to be able to reach the St. Lawrence River?

The Hébert Family of New France

The Hébert family were the first French farmers to settle in New France. A daughter in the Hébert family could have written a story this way. What qualities did the Hébert family have that helped them set a good example for the other farmers?

My name is Guillemette Hébert. My family was the first to come to New France to farm. We had to struggle at first, but in time we made a good life for ourselves.

My father, Louis Hébert, was trained as a druggist and doctor, but he always loved farming. We went to live at Port-Royal when it was first built, but we returned to France when the first settlement there failed. In 1617, Champlain invited Father to come to Québec. We sold our house in Paris and sailed back across the Atlantic Ocean to our new home.

My father had hoped to be given six hectares of land for our new farm, but we were only given three. The fur-trading company made us sell everything we grew to them at the prices they set. They also made Father spend most of his time treating the sick people in Québec. The traders would not let Father try to trade with any of the Aboriginal Peoples to make extra money.

Louis Hébert, his wife, and their three children were the first French settlers to support themselves by farming.

We all worked hard to get our farm started. We had only an axe, a pick, and a shovel with which to clear the land, but we were soon planting crops. Champlain encouraged us. The other fur traders did nothing to help.

My mother, Marie, started classes for Aboriginal children who lived nearby.

Father died in 1627 from injuries he got when he fell on the ice. Mother stayed in New France and kept our farm going.

I was married by that time. My husband and I helped Mother. We all stayed on the farm, even when the English captured Québec in 1629. We rejoiced when Québec was returned to France four years later. We were sure New France would grow and prosper.

France and England Compete for Canada

By the middle of the 1700s, France and England had had a series of wars with each other. The two countries had been rivals in Europe long before they fought to control North America. The two countries often competed with each other to control settlements in different parts of the world.

England and France had competed over North America for almost a century. Both countries wanted to expand their settlements in North America. There were many battles between the French and English. Some parts of Canada, such as the settlement at Port-Royal, changed hands several times.

By 1750, there were about 70 000 French people living in New France and Acadia. Most of the French settlers lived along the St. Lawrence River. French fur traders had also explored the land west and south of the Great Lakes. They claimed that area for France and built forts and trading posts along lakes and rivers to defend it.

Most of the English settlers lived along the Atlantic coast of North America, south of Acadia. The two million English settlers wanted more land to build new settlements. They wanted to move west and north to find more farmland. These areas were claimed by the French, however, and the English found their way blocked by the French forts.

Finding Information

1. What were some of the reasons France and England competed for control of Canada?

2. How could the English find a way to build more settlements farther west?

A number of battles were fought between the English and French during the Seven Years' War. The battle on the Plains of Abraham in 1759 is known as the Seige of Québec. This battle helped England win the war.

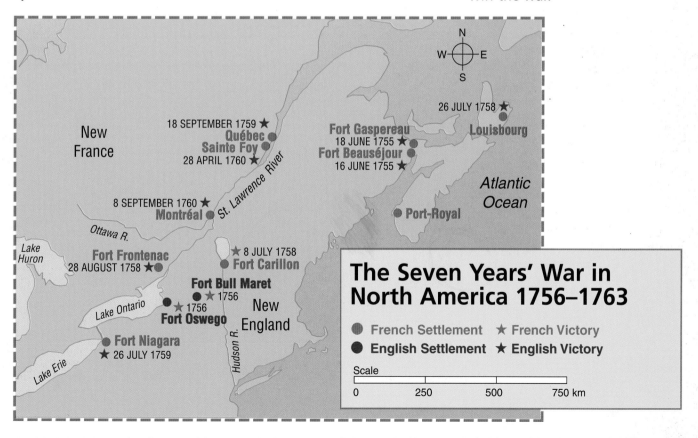

The Seven Years' War in North America 1756–1763

● French Settlement ★ French Victory
● English Settlement ★ English Victory

Scale

0   250   500   750 km

The Fall of New France

Time Line

- **1754**
  French and English begin fighting in North America

- **1756**
  Britain declares war and the Seven Years' War begins

- **1757**
  French win important battles

- **1758**
  English capture Louisbourg and war shifts

- **1759**
  Siege of Québec, France loses

- **1763**
  Treaty of Paris, English gain control of North America

What do you think?

Why was Québec an important settlement to control?

Québec was conquered by the English in 1759 in a battle on the Plains of Abraham. The English army was led by General James Wolfe, who died in the battle.

The final struggle for North America began in 1755. Soldiers from English settlements attacked four French forts. They were only able to capture one, Fort Beauséjour. In 1756, the English attacked again. Once more they were beaten by the French. In 1756, the Seven Years' War had started in Europe, and this added to the conflict in North America.

Although the French were winning at first, they had problems. They had few soldiers and not enough supplies. Fighting took people away from their farms, so food became scarce. The French government sent the Marquis of Montcalm to help, but he argued with local officials at Québec.

In 1758, the English began to win victories. England had a powerful navy and sent many troops to North America. They captured Louisbourg and Fort Frontenac, which opened the way up the St. Lawrence. In the summer of 1759, a large English force sailed up the river. They landed near Québec but could not enter the city because of Montcalm's defences. On September 13, they discovered a secret path up the cliffs near Québec. All through the night, the English soldiers quietly moved along this path. When the sun rose, the English army was lined up just outside the walls of the city on the Plains of Abraham.

Montcalm quickly organized his men and marched out to fight, but his best soldiers could not be found in time. The French fought bravely, but many were killed, including Montcalm. Those left alive retreated to the city and surrendered. Soon after, the other French settlements surrendered to the English. The Seven Years' War ended in 1763. The Treaty of Paris was signed, and France gave up its claim to land in Canada.

What Should the English Do?

When the Seven Years' War began in 1756, there were only 70 000 French settlers in Acadia and New France, compared to the two million English settlers in Canada and south along the Atlantic coast. When England won control of all the French territory in Canada, the English leaders had to decide how to govern the French people. They had several choices.

CHOICES	QUESTIONS
The English could force all the French to leave their homes in Canada. They had tried this in Nova Scotia in 1755. It caused much hardship and made the Acadians angry. There were about six times as many French along the St. Lawrence River as there had been in Nova Scotia.	Where could the English leaders send so many people? How could they move them?
The English could force the French to become more like themselves. They could make the French learn to speak English. They could make them **worship** as Protestants rather than as Roman Catholics. They could divide the seigneuries into square farms like the English settlers' farms.	How would the French react to such a plan? What if they asked France for help?
The English could bring more English settlers to Canada. They could bring in enough English settlers to outnumber the French. These settlers could set up farms, schools, and churches like those in England.	How could the English leaders get settlers to agree to come? Where would they find land for them?
The English could let the French people of Canada keep their own way of life. They could make English laws to take the place of some French laws, but let the French keep their own language, way of life, and Catholic religion.	Would the French settlers accept laws made by the English? What problems might be caused by letting the French keep their language, way of life, and religion?

Which choice or choices do you think the English should make?
What are your reasons?

The Coming of the Loyalists

Time Line

1763
English law passed preventing settlers from moving west

1775
American War of Independence begins. Migration to Canada

1783
War of Independence ends. Second wave of Loyalists move to Canada

1784
Nova Scotia is divided into two colonies. Many Loyalists settle in New Brunswick.

1789
Loyalists granted honour by the Governor to bear the initials U.E. for Unity of Empire

1791
Quebec is divided into Upper and Lower Canada.

Find out

What problems might have occurred between the Loyalists and the French?

Some of the Loyalists sailed up the coast to their new homes in Canada. Others travelled by land, camping in the woods on their way north.

After the Treaty of Paris was signed, the English renamed New France Quebec, after Champlain's settlement. In 1774, they passed the Quebec Act, which let the French in Quebec keep their language, religion, and some laws. Only a few English and Scottish merchants moved to Quebec. These merchants soon took control of the fur trade in Montréal and Québec City.

The English wanted more English settlers to move to Quebec. They passed a law in 1763 that prevented settlers on the Atlantic coast south of Acadia from moving west. The West was supposed to be left to the Aboriginal Peoples as hunting grounds.

The English settlers on the coast were unhappy with this law. They wanted to move west, not north. The settlements decided to break away from England. Fighting began between the settlers and English troops in 1775. The American War of Independence lasted until 1783. It ended with the birth of a new country, the United States of America.

Some English settlers remained loyal to England during the War of Independence. Many of these **Loyalists** came north to Quebec and Nova Scotia. Some members of the League of the Iroquois were also Loyalists. They came north to Quebec as well. The government promised every Loyalist at least 40 hectares of land. The coming of the Loyalists changed Canada. Many settled in New Brunswick, which became a province in 1784 when Nova Scotia was divided. In 1791, a law divided Quebec into two provinces called Lower Canada and Upper Canada. Upper Canada later became Ontario, and Lower Canada became the province of Quebec.

Most of the French-speaking people lived in Lower Canada. They were able to keep some French laws because of the Quebec Act. Most of the English-speaking people settled in Upper Canada. They wanted English laws and the English way of dividing land.

A Young Loyalist Remembers

After the American War of Independence, many settlers remained loyal to England. These Loyalists decided to move north to settle in the territory still controlled by England. Some of the Loyalists wrote about these events in diaries, letters, and journals. This is how an eleven-year-old girl might have described her move to Canada. Whose land did the Loyalist settlers take? How would they have changed the Aboriginal Peoples' way of life?

Father said we were going to move north to a new home in the English settlements there. A ship was ready to take us, so our whole family hurried to get ready.

We killed our cow and sold the meat. A neighbour took home the fat from the cow. She made us a parcel of candles from the fat with plenty of beeswax in them to make them good and hard.

Uncle harvested our wheat. Grandmother came to visit and made bags for the grain. We had twenty bags to sell.

We packed a tub of butter, a tub of pickles, and a good supply of potatoes. We also packed our warmest clothes.

Then, on Tuesday, our house was suddenly surrounded by rebel soldiers. They took Father away as a prisoner. Uncle asked them to let Father go. He promised to see that Father appeared before them in the morning. They took Father away anyway. I cried all night. When morning came, they let Father go free. I guess they couldn't think of a reason to keep him any longer.

We had five wagonloads of things carried down the Hudson River on a small boat. At New York, we boarded the big sailing ship that would take us to Saint John. I was just eleven years old when we left our farm to come to Canada.

On the trip, some people became sick. Several babies were born on the ship.

It was a cold and crowded journey. Life was very hard after we landed. We had to live in tents that the government gave us. The government also gave us some flour, butter, pork, and farming tools.

The melting snow and the rain soaked into our beds on the ground of the tent. Mother got so chilled that she became ill. She was never very well after that. We lived in a tent at St. Anne's until Father built us a house. Later, St. Anne's was named Fredericton. Father looked around the lot of land we had received from the government until he found a fresh spring of water. He stooped down and pulled away the fallen leaves that covered it and tasted the water. It was very good, so he picked a spot nearby to build our house.

One morning when we woke up, we found snow lying all around our tent. Father came wading through the snow and told us the house was ready. There was no floor, no glass in the windows, and no door, but we had a roof at least. A good fire was blazing in the fireplace. Mother made a big loaf of bread. She boiled a kettle of water and put a piece of the bread in a metal bowl. We toasted the bread and ate our breakfast.

Mother said, "Thank goodness we no longer live in fear of having shots fired through our house. This is the best meal I have tasted for many a day."

Lumber Settlements along the Ottawa River

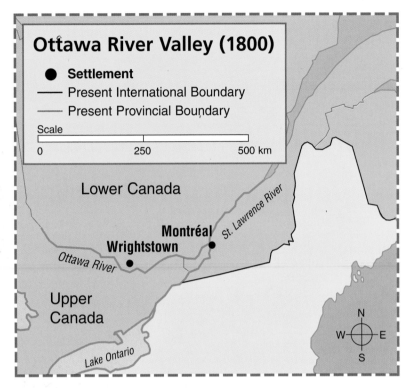

Ottawa River Valley (1800)

- ● Settlement
- — Present International Boundary
- — Present Provincial Boundary

Scale
0   250   500 km

Lower Canada

Montréal
Wrightstown

St. Lawrence River

Ottawa River

Upper Canada

Lake Ontario

N
W E
S

In the late 1700s, many English-speaking settlers arrived in Canada. All the farmland along the St. Lawrence River was settled, so the new settlers had to find land somewhere else.

Some of the newcomers settled in the Ottawa River valley. These settlers found large forests of pine and oak near Chaudière Falls on the Ottawa River. Philemon Wright started the lumber industry there. He took the first raft of **timbers**, called the *Colombo*, down the Ottawa River to Montréal to sell in 1806. By 1820, 1 000 people worked in the lumber industry at Wrightstown. People came from Scotland, Ireland, and the United States. There were also French Canadians. All had come to work in the forests and sawmills, and the new settlements that grew.

Before the Ottawa River was used to take timbers to Montréal, it was used as a fur-trading route.

Philemon Wright settled the town of Wrightstown to build a lumber mill. It later became known as Hull, Quebec.

Each year, a timber drive began when the ice melted. First, logs cut in the forest were pushed into the river. They plunged down the river to the sawmill. The loggers ran along the banks with long poles, pushing the logs out into the river current to keep them moving.

At the sawmill, logs were collected and then cut into timbers. To take these timbers down river to sell, they were lashed together into small rafts called cribs. The cribs were joined together to form a huge raft. On the raft, the loggers built **bunkhouses** and a fire pit for cooking. Long oars were attached to the sides to steer the raft. Sails were used when the wind was blowing down river.

To get the raft through the rapids, it was taken apart and each crib was guided through on its own. Sometimes the loggers built wooden **chutes**, like slides, over rapids or falls. Then they did not have to separate the cribs. They could send the whole raft over the rapids.

When the rafts reached the markets at Montréal or Québec, the loggers were paid. They went back to their homes or farms until the next logging season.

Life in a logging camp was not easy. Meals were almost always the same. Loggers ate beans, bread, and strong tea, even for breakfast. Their clothing was warm and hard-wearing. It had to last the winter, because there was no place to buy more. The loggers' winter home was often a large log cabin or **shanty**. Shanties were put up quickly and were used for only one season. Inside the shanty, bunks were built around the walls. The beds were made of spruce boughs.

What do you think?

Imagine you are a logger on the Ottawa River. Describe what might have happened during a timber drive.

Timber slides were built over rapids so the cribs of logs could pass over them easily.

The Wright Family

This story might have been told by a member of the Wright family. It describes how Philemon Wright started the lumber industry in the Ottawa River valley. Why was the valley attractive to settlers? How would cutting down large numbers of trees change the Aboriginal Peoples' way of life?

My father, Philemon Wright, was the man who started the lumber industry in the Ottawa River valley. That was not his first plan, but that was what ended up happening.

I was born in Massachusetts in the United States. We lived there until I was ten years old. My father always talked of taking us away from such a crowded place to a farm in the wilderness. He travelled to many places looking for the best spot for us to settle. Finally, he decided on the Chaudière Falls area on the Ottawa River.

Our whole family moved to the new settlement in the winter of 1800 with five other families who wanted to leave Massachusetts. As soon as it got warm, we began to clear the land for gardens and to build small log cabins.

Father knew it would be several years before we would have enough grain to sell. He convinced some of the other settlers to help him cut timber in the winter months when they were not farming. There was a good market for wood.

We used the river as a way to get the timber to Montréal or Québec for sale. We built chutes over the rapids and falls. I loved to ride on the rafts as they shot along the river.

The lumber industry grew so fast that soon more people worked in it than at farming. Father was disappointed. He really wanted to see all the families farming the land.

Philemon Wright delivered the first raft of timbers, called the *Colombo*, to Montréal. From there, they were shipped to England.

In Summary

1. England and France built settlements in early Canada. The settlers learned how to live in the new land. They met Aboriginal Peoples who lived near their homes.

2. The first English settlements were in Newfoundland. Some fishers began to spend the winters there in the 1500s. Soon there were permanent fishing settlements.

3. The French built settlements in Acadia on the Atlantic coast, and in New France along the St. Lawrence River. The Acadians and the settlers of New France became farmers because these areas had rich soil suited for growing crops.

4. England and France competed to control the settlements in Canada. Acadia passed back and forth between the English and French many times. From 1756 to 1763, England and France fought the Seven Years' War. At the end of the war, England controlled all of the European settlements in Canada. England decided the French could keep their language, religion, way of life, and many laws.

5. After the English settlements south of Canada won independence from England, many settlers from there moved to Canada because they remained loyal to England. The Loyalists moved to the east coast and to the Great Lakes area to settle. Some of the Iroquois south of the Great Lakes were Loyalists. They also moved to Canada.

6. As the settlements grew, new industries began. The lumber industry became important, along with the older industries of fishing, farming, and the fur trade.

7. The English named new provinces, including Quebec and New Brunswick. Later they divided Quebec into Upper and Lower Canada.

Reliving the Past

1. The English leaders let the French settlers in Canada keep their own language, way of life, and some of their laws. Was this a good way to solve the problems between the French and the English people of early Canada? Why or why not?

2. How did their solution help bring about two official languages in Canada today?

3. Use your library to research what life is like in a logging camp today. Compare this life with life in the logging camps of early Canada. What differences can you find? What things are the same?

Conclusion

Aboriginal Peoples, explorers, fur traders, missionaries, and settlers all lived in early Canada. This book has described how all these people interacted and learned from one another. It has shown how contact with other groups changed each group's way of life.

Aboriginal Peoples lived here long before the Europeans arrived. Each of the Aboriginal groups had its own way of life based on the resources of the area where they lived. Aboriginal groups traded and visited with one another.

In the late 1400s, Europeans began to search for a new sea route to Asia. Some explorers sailed west across the Atlantic Ocean where they found North America. The explorers were looking for the Northwest Passage to Asia, but they became interested in the resources and peoples of Canada.

About 1500, Europeans began coming to North America regularly. The Europeans met the Aboriginal Peoples and learned how to live in the new land. The Aboriginal Peoples observed the European way of life and learned many new things.

The Europeans began the Newfoundland fishery and the fur trade. The fur traders also explored farther inland. They developed fur-trading partnerships with the Aboriginal Peoples they met. The Aboriginal Peoples helped the Europeans. The Aboriginal Peoples showed the Europeans their maps and acted as guides. They also showed the Europeans how to use canoes to travel Canada's many waterways.

Aboriginal Peoples lived in sophisticated communities before the Europeans arrived. They had their own ways to trade, govern, and live among one another.

How did the interaction between the Aboriginal Peoples and Europeans change the ways they lived?

Missionaries came to the new land with the fur traders and settlers. They wanted to teach their beliefs to the Aboriginal Peoples. They built missions in Aboriginal territories. The missionaries left many records that can help us learn about the past.

The first European settlers came to Canada toward the beginning of the 1600s. They had learned that Canada had many resources, and thought it would be a good place to live. Some of the first settlers were fishers, fur traders, and missionaries. Soon other people came. They started farms and towns. They also began a lumber industry.

Madame Champlain taught Aboriginal children around 1620 in the settlement of Québec.

Fur traders were the first Europeans to explore the West.

French voyageurs often had to canoe through dangerous rapids to trade their furs.

Missionaries built Sainte-Marie in Huronia to teach the Huron about Christian ways of life.

What did the Europeans learn from the Aboriginal Peoples?
What did the Aboriginal Peoples learn from the Europeans?

French settlers lived in Acadia and New France. The English lived in Newfoundland, near Hudson Bay, and south of Acadia. The French and English settlers met the Aboriginal groups who lived near the settlements.

The French and English began to compete for control of the new land. In 1713, the English won control over part of Acadia. They expelled the Acadians from their homes because they feared that the Acadians would not be loyal to England. In 1763, the English won the Seven Years' War. This gave them control over all the French and English areas in Canada. There were many Aboriginal and French people living in these areas. The English, French, and Aboriginal Peoples had to find ways to live and work together.

This habitant family of New France held land under the seigneurial system. Habitants had a different way of farming than the Loyalists. Habitants farmed land that was divided into long strips rather than square hectares.

This engraving by R. Paton shows the English and French in battle on July 1, 1758. The *Prudent* was burned and the *Bienfaisant* was taken over by the English in the Louisbourg harbour.

What types of interaction might there be in a country with French, Aboriginal, and English people living in it?

As time passed, many new people came to live in Canada. Some came from Europe and others came from the United States. They joined the early settlers and Aboriginal Peoples who already lived in Canada.

Throughout this book, there have been many stories about people who lived in early Canada. The stories show competition, conflict, and co-operation among Canada's early people. The stories help us understand Canada today.

These Loyalists are finding out what land they would be given from the government.

Settlers in the Ottawa River valley took their timber to mills where it was cut and taken down the river to be sold.

Why might settlers want to settle in one area more than another?
What are some reasons settlers came to Canada?

Glossary

Aboriginal Peoples: the first people who lived in Canada, and those who are descended from them, including First Nations, Inuit, and Metis

Acadia: an area where French settlers lived on Canada's east coast, including Nova Scotia, Prince Edward Island, and part of New Brunswick

Algonquian: a group of related Aboriginal languages, including the Mi'kmaq and Cree languages

ancestor: a relative who lived a long time ago

anthropologist: a person who studies the way different groups of people live

archaeologist: a person who studies the things left by people who lived long ago

archive: a place where old records are stored

Arctic: the region around the North Pole

artifact: any object made by human beings

band: a small group of Aboriginal families that live and travel together

baptize: a Christian ceremony admitting a person to the Church and cleansing his or her sins

bilge: the area under the floor of a ship's hold

brier: a thorny bush, such as a wild rose

bunkhouse: a building lined with bunkbeds where workers sleep

century: a time period of one hundred years

chapel: a small building used as a church

chute: a wooden slide built in a river to carry goods over rapids and waterfalls

climate: the normal weather of a place

convent: a building where a group of religious women, or nuns, live

coureur de bois: an early French fur trader who travelled to the homes of the Aboriginal Peoples to trade

cove: a small, protected bay on a coast

crew: all the people who work on a ship

decade: a period of ten years

diet: the kind of food and drink that a person usually has from day to day

dike: a type of wall built to keep the ocean away from a low piece of land

disease: an illness

elder: an old and respected member of a community

epidemic: when a large number of people catch the same illness

evidence: clues that help us find out what happened

explore: to travel over land or water to find out about new places and the people who live there

fishery: an area where fish are caught, such as the Grand Banks

flax: a plant used to produce oil and which is made into cloth called linen

foreigner: a person from a country other than your own

fortress: a large, well-protected fort

fur trade: an industry in which Europeans traded their goods for furs with the Aboriginal Peoples of Canada

Grand Banks: a fishing area southeast of Newfoundland

gulf: an arm of an ocean that goes into the land

habitant: a French settler who lived on a farm

harbour: a place on a coast or river that is a good place for ships to dock

historian: a person who studies the events and people of the past

hold: a storage area below the deck of a ship

instrument: a tool that helps get something done

Inuit: some groups of Aboriginal people who live mainly in the north

Inuk: one Inuit person

Iroquoian: a group of related Aboriginal languages, including the Huron and Iroquois languages

kayak: an Inuit boat made of hide stretched over a light frame

lacrosse: a game first played by the Aboriginal Peoples of eastern Canada, in which teams play with rackets and balls

landmark: usually a feature of the land, such as a mountain, that is easily seen and can be used as a guide

league: a number of people or nations who join together to help one another

lowland: land that is lower and flatter than the neighbouring land

Loyalist: a person loyal to the English monarch who moved to Canada from the United States after the American War of Independence

lumber: logs, boards, and other wood products roughly prepared for use

manitou: a Cree term meaning great spirit

marshland: a low, wet area

martyr: a person who dies or suffers because of religious beliefs

merchant: a person who buys goods and sells them for a higher price

Methodist: one kind of Protestant church of the Christian religion

missionary: a person who tries to teach religious beliefs to people who do not already share them

monarch: the queen or king of a country

mortar and pestle: a mortar is a type of bowl, and a pestle is a tool used to grind foods in the bowl into paste or powder

musket: an old type of gun

mutiny: when the crew of a ship unlawfully takes control from the captain

neutral: taking neither side in a fight or an argument

New France: the area the French settled along the St. Lawrence River and around the Great Lakes

Northwest Passage: a route to Asia that Europeans hoped to find by sailing northwest across the Atlantic Ocean

nun: a religious woman who lives in a convent and dedicates her life to the Church

oath: a promise

outfit: provide with supplies such as food and clothing

palisade: a high fence of poles or stakes built to protect an area from attack

peace pipe: a long tobacco pipe used in Aboriginal peace-making ceremonies

pelt: the skin of a fur-bearing animal

pemmican: a kind of food made from dried meat mixed with fat and sometimes berries

peninsula: a piece of land almost surrounded by water

permanent: something made to last a long time

petroglyph: a picture carved into rock

portage: a place where travellers had to carry their boats across the land from one lake or river to another

priest: a minister authorized to carry out ceremonies in certain Christian churches

Protestant: a branch of the Christian religion that has several different kinds of churches

rapids: part of a river where the water rushes quickly, usually over rocks

raw materials: natural resources that can be made into useful goods

record: writing done for use in the future

religious order: group of religious people who follow the same way of life

reserve: land set aside for use by Aboriginal Peoples

resources: things that can be used to meet needs

rival: a person or group who competes with someone else for the same thing

Roman Catholic: one branch of the Christian religion

sagamité: corn soup eaten by the Huron

saint: a person recognized as a religious hero

scurvy: a disease caused by lack of Vitamin C

seigneur: a landowner in the St. Lawrence River valley who was granted land by the king of France

settler: a person who goes to live in a new part of the world

shaman: an Aboriginal religious person, a medicine man

shanty: a rough, log building where loggers lived

Sieur: the title Sir, in French

smallpox: a disease that results in high fever and skin blisters

snare: a trap made to catch small animals

spice: seasonings obtained from plants that flavour other foods

stable: a building where animals are kept

strait: a narrow passage of water connecting two larger bodies of water

structure: something that has been built

tax: money paid to support a community

timber: logs trimmed into a square shape

toll: a charge for a service

translate: to change from one language to another

treaty: an agreement between nations

Ursuline: a Roman Catholic order of nuns who teach and care for the sick and needy

voyage: a journey by sea or water

voyageur: a French fur trader who was licenced to trade with the Aboriginal Peoples

weir: a fence of stakes or broken branches put in water to catch fish

wigwam: a kind of Aboriginal home made of bark or hide over a frame made of poles

wintering partner: a fur trader who lived among the Aboriginal Peoples and traded for furs during the winter, then met his partner from the city, who took the furs away to sell

worship: to take part in religious ceremonies

Picture Credits

Cover: Carte du Canada ou de la Nouvelle France, by Claude and Guillaume Delisle, 1703, issued in 1730 by Corens and Mortier. Reproduced courtesy the National Map Collection, National Archives of Canada; p. 4: (right) National Archives of Canada (NAC) C-5933, (left) Lee Updike; p. 5: (top left) NAC C-1020, (top right) NAC C-73422, (bottom left) National Library NL-5369; p. 6: (top) NAC C-113345, (bottom) National Museums of Canada (NMC); p.8: NMC-40461; p. 9: Digital Vision Ltd. 028455; p. 12: (top) Marquis of Lorne Collection, (bottom) Architect of The Capitol, Rice Gatherers, p. 14: (top) Glenbow Archives, Calgary, Alberta, AF900, (bottom) Glenbow Archives, R84.16; p. 22: courtesy of the Royal Ontario Museum, Toronto, Canada; p. 26: Glenbow Archives NA-1344-3; p. 30: Rogers Cantel, Inc.; p. 31: NAC C-70249; p. 32: Rogers Cantel, Inc.; p. 35: NAC C-12235; p. 36: NAC C-11413; p. 37: British Museum No. 117a; p. 38: NAC C-13320; p. 39: Rogers Cantel, Inc.; p. 41: NAC C-17727; p. 42: Public Archives of Canada C-2061; p.44: (left) NMC 59502, (right) Dave Taylor 95018; p. 45: NAC C-17338; p. 48: (top) NAC C-09892, (bottom) NAC C-3165; p. 50: NAC C-2774; p. 51: NAC C-1918; p. 52: NAC C-1917; p. 53: Rogers Cantel, Inc.; p. 54: Royal Ontario Museum; p. 55: Hudson's Bay Company Archives, Provincial Archives of Manitoba, HBCA P-417; p. 56: NAC C-6896; p. 57: NAC C-16859; p. 58: NAC C-8711; p. 59: NAC C-2773; p 60: courtesy Environment Canada, Canadian Parks Service; p. 61: Glenbow Archives NA-1532-1; p. 62: NAC; p. 63: NAC C-18858; p. 64: National Gallery of Canada #6663; p. 65: (top) Canadian Heritage, Parks Canada, Laird Niven, (bottom) Canadian Heritage, Parks Canada, Brian Molyneaux; p. 67: NAC C-21404; p. 70: NAC C-8070; p. 71: NAC C-14360; p. 72: NAC C-12340; p. 73: NAC C-4765; p. 74: courtesy Victoria University Library (Toronto); p. 75: courtesy The Champlain Society; p. 76: NAC C-40597; p. 78: NAC C-3686; p. 80: NAC C-98232; p. 81: Novia Scotia Museum; p. 82: (top) NAC C-5907, (bottom) Corel Corporation 230082; p. 84: (top) NAC C-9711, (bottom) National Gallery of Canada #6275; p. 86: NAC C-16952; p. 88: NAC C-1078; p. 90: NAC C-73449; p. 92: NAC C-608; p. 93: NAC C-43647 p. 94: NAC C-73702; p. 96: NMC J4436; p. 97: (top left) NAC C-1410, (top right) Hudson's Bay Company, Provincial Archives of Canada HBCA P-415, (bottom left) Canadian Pacific Corporate Archives, (bottom right) Rogers Cantel, Inc.; p. 98: (top) NAC C-96362, (bottom) NAC C-7111; p. 99: (top) Arts Associates, (bottom) NAC C-11200.

Text Credits

p.15, "How the Good Spirits Came to Rule the World" adapted from Kirbyson/McCreath/Skeoch, *Discovering Canada: Settling a Land,* Prentice-Hall Canada Inc., 1982, pp. 50-51; p. 23, "Growing Corn" chart adapted from *Canadian Vanishing Communities: Cultivators and Traders of the Eastern Woodlands* by Winnifred Ferry. © 1980 GLC Publishers Ltd; p. 27, "Reliving the Past" adapted from *Canadian Vanishing Communities: Cultivators and Traders of the Eastern Woodlands* by Winnifred Ferry. © 1980 GLC Publishers Ltd; pp. 32-33, Cartier's Journal entries adapted from H.P. Biggar, *The Voyages of Jacques Cartier,* reproduced and adapted with the permission of the Minister of Supply and Services Canada; p. 49, versions of Adam Dollard story adapted from Kirbyson/McCreath/Skeoch, *Discovering Canada: Settling a Land,* Prentice-Hall Canada Inc., 1982, p. 31; p. 51, HBC prices and questions adapted from *James Marsh, New Beginnings, Vol 1,* reprinted with permission of McClelland & Stewart, the Canadian Publisher; p. 68, The Huron Carol reprinted from *Folk Songs of Canada,* Edith Fowke and Richard Johnston, published by Waterloo Music Company Ltd; p. 69, the destruction of Huronia adapted from the *Jesuit Relations.*

Index